RESISTING TYRANNY:
A Christian Response to Government Overreach

Collected works by
TOBIAS RIEMENSCHNEIDER

Including an article by
DR. JOHN MACARTHUR

And a foreword by
DR. JAMES WHITE

Ezra Press

Pastor Tobias has served the church tremendously well in thinking both clearly and robustly concerning all that has taken place in recent times. He has also demonstrated the kind of pastoral graciousness that is so needed in addressing such difficult matters, providing the kind of leadership and pastoral care that have been so lacking. Should the church in Germany and abroad take her queue from him, she will press on both resolvedly and triumphantly in faithfulness to her Lord. I believe the content of this work will have lasting relevance for many years to come. May the head of the church, the Lord Jesus Christ, increase the influence of Pastor Tobias in both Germany and beyond, for the glory of God!

– Dr. James Coates
Pastor of GraceLife Church, Edmonton, Alberta, Canada

In this book Tobias Riemenschneider articulates truth that must be heard by the church today. The worldwide reaction to COVID-19 has forced the church to go back to the word and crystalize the role of church and state, and how they relate to one another. I'm convinced that the contents of this book will serve the church well as the western world continues in its rebellion against God. May you be blessed and Christ be magnified through this work.

– Tim Stephens
Pastor of Fairview Baptist Church, Calgary, Alberta, Canada

Pastor Tobias Riemenschneider's work is the burst of a golden flare across the black languishing night of European apostasy. May this awaken the European continent towards a new reformation and revival, as she desperately needs.

– Jacob Reaume
Pastor of Trinity Bible Chapel, Waterloo, Ontario, Canada

The Covid season uncovered a pre-existing deep divide in the fundamental commitments and assumptions of Western Christians. Although the shunning and cancelling of leaders resisting state overreach was a sadly common theme, one of my greatest joys of the past few years has been to meet and have fellowship with pastors and leaders whose lives and ministries testify to the conviction that Jesus Christ is Lord of all, is absolute Head of His church, and the ruler of the kings of the earth. Pastor Tobias Riemenschneider is one such man. This work is both insightful and scriptural, but Tobias is no armchair theologian. His record of faithful, courageous leadership in standing for Christian liberty and shepherding the people under his care give added weight to his challenging words. I commend this book to you.

– Rev. Dr. Joseph Boot
Founder and President, Ezra Institute

Over these past few years, we have witnessed an unprecedented display of tyranny all over the world. In the West, many of us assumed our way of life was immune to such draconian measures. We were wrong. Lockdowns, masking, and vaccine mandates became the norm. It has been immensely challenging to take a stand in America. It was all but impossible to take a stand in Germany. Tobias Riemenschneider is one of the only Christian pastors who refused to comply. His biblical exegesis and application regarding Covid represents the best material I've read on the subject.

– Joel Webbon
President of Right Response Ministries;
Senior Pastor of Covenant Bible Church, Georgetown, Texas

We are living through a period of church history where the vast majority of local churches and denominations have followed the counsel of the world and looked to adapt Scripture accordingly. The alarming misinterpretation and misapplication of topics such as the role of government and 'love your neighbor' has left Christians around the world disillusioned and spiritually abandoned by their leaders, in a time when they needed them to stand up the most. This is why I am thankful for my dear brother and friend, Tobias, who has put together this excellent resource filled with Biblical truth in relation to this Covid situation, which is also a testimony of its application in the life of his church.

– John-William Noble
Pastor of Grace Baptist Church, Aberdeen, Scotland, U.K.

Published by Ezra Press
P.O. Box 9, STN Main, Grimsby, Ontario, Canada L3M 4G1
© 2023 Tobias Riemenschneider. All rights reserved. This book may not be reproduced, in whole or in part, without written permission from the publishers.

Unless otherwise indicated, Scripture quotations are from the ESV® Bible (The Holy Bible, English Standard Version®). Copyright © 2001 by Crossway, a publishing ministry of Good News Publishers. Used by permission.

All rights reserved.

Book design by Rachel Eras

Printed in the United States of America

ISBN: 978-1-989169-24-7

Contents

Foreword	9
About this Book	13
Keeping Jesus in the Center – Precisely Because of Corona	23
Submission and Resistance	41
Guidance for a Biblical Approach to the Covid Vaccines	75
Mandatory Vaccination and the Christian Conscience – an Urgent Plea	101
Looking Back on Two Years of Covid	107
Frankfurt Declaration of Christian and Civil Liberties	133
'Christians Against the Abuse of Power': Theologians Around the World Sign Statement Rejecting Government Lockdowns	143
Why I Signed the Frankfurt Declaration	153
Why the Frankfurt Declaration Is Necessary	159
(How to) Love Your Neighbor – The BioLogos Statement vs. The Frankfurt Declaration: Two Opposite Evangelical Responses to the State's Power	171
Address at the "Church at War" Conference in Waterloo, ON, Canada	179

Foreword
Dr. James White

In the providence of God, I began fellowshipping with the fine folks at the Reformed Baptist Church of Frankfurt, Germany, during my world travels. For a number of years, I visited the church annually. Then the Covid pandemic hit, and everything changed. I continued my relationship at a distance, teaching church history classes on a regular basis via the Internet.

This allowed me to keep up to date with the challenges the saints were facing in Germany. I realized quickly that I was deeply blessed to live in the United States. I learned firsthand about the draconian actions of the German government from men and women I considered dear and precious. I had to pray regularly for them, and at the same time, to give thanks for my freedoms, though I well knew many in my own country wanted to be just as severe in their actions as the German government.

Tobias Riemenschneider together with his fellow pastor Peter Schild had to struggle with the many questions that faced the church in the West for the first time in our lives. We spoke often, and I did all I could to be of encouragement, including reading drafts of statements, providing what guidance or help I could. I am one of the pastors of Apologia Church in Mesa, Arizona, and we made the decision at the beginning to not shut down but to continue meeting for worship. We addressed our reasons from the pulpit, and sought to encourage others struggling with the same challenges.

Over the past few years Tobias has led the believing, church-based, Christ-exalting movement in Germany and, in these pages, he provides a summary of the reasoning and argumentation he and his church have been presenting to the broader Christian community. They have received a tremendous amount of resistance, which is hardly surprising. We all sense that there will be more challenges ahead. But we must take the time now to lay a firm foundation before the waters of persecution and trouble rise again.

The American church has been an encouragement to our brothers overseas, but likewise, we have much to learn from them as well. May Tobias' conclusions, hammered out on the anvil of distressing times in Germany, provide light and insight to all of us as we seek to honor Christ in all that we do.

– Dr. James White
Pastor of Apologia Church, Mesa, Arizona, USA;
Director of Alpha and Omega Ministries

About this Book
Tobias Riemenschneider

THIS BOOK IS A COMPILATION of statements, sermons, lectures, etc., that I wrote or gave, or at least played a significant role in writing, regarding the restrictive state measures during the Covid crisis and the response of a large part of the church in this regard. This book was first published in German. And even though many of the contributions printed in this book come from a German context, I am confident that they will also be useful for Christians from other countries, because the fundamental problems we face are the same everywhere. I am therefore exceedingly grateful to Dr. Joe Boot and the brothers of Ezra Press for publishing this book in English. For a better understanding, I would like to briefly explain in advance the context in which the respective texts were created.

The state measures during the Covid era were unprecedented in the history of the Federal Republic of Germany. Never before had the state infringed so massively, and for so long, on virtually all the fundamental rights of citizens – with still incalculable consequences. The state revealed itself to be authoritarian and repressive in a way that had seemed unimaginable in the Western world. All the more shocking was the reaction of most churches: Largely uncritically, they obeyed the state orders, from distancing, masking, and testing mandates to bans on worship, singing, and the ordinances. But, as if that were not enough, a number of pastors, Bible scholars and seminary professors were found, calling on Christians to submit to the state's measures, claiming that this was their biblical duty.

In Germany, for example, more than fifty men, some of them very respected, published the thesis paper "Keeping Jesus in the Center – Despite Corona," in which they appealed to Scripture to legitimize the state's injustice and called on Christians to submit to whatever measures the state imposed. The statement "Keeping Jesus in the Center – Precisely Because of Corona" (Part 1 of this book), which my co-pastor Peter Schild and I published on March 9, 2021, is opposed to this thesis paper and aims to provide Christians with a biblical argumentation against the theologically and exegetically deficient statements of the thesis paper and, thus, to assist them pastorally.

The key biblical passage cited by the advocates of subordination to the state's measures, and which we therefore also had to deal with in depth, are the first verses of the thirteenth chapter of Paul's letter to the Romans. It is astonishing how these verses were repeatedly misinterpreted (consciously or unconsciously), not only in the Covid era but also in history, to justify unconditional obedience to the state. The sermon "Submission and Resistance" (Part 2 of this book), which I preached on March 21, 2021, therefore interprets these and related Scripture passages in detail and shows both the scope and the limits of the biblical command to submit to the state. I have deliberately refrained from adapting the wording of the sermon too much for the printed version. The printed version thus corresponds, apart from minor changes, to what was actually preached, because I want to preserve the character as a sermon, even if this means that some formulations are unusual for a written version.

About This Book

Towards the end of 2021, the situation in Germany came to a head. Politicians and the media – and thus most of society – had settled on the idea that "the unvaccinated" were to blame for the spread of infection and the "no-alternative" measures taken by the state. Hatred of the new scapegoats was propagated ever more blatantly by politicians and the media. They were vilified as science-deniers and conspiracy theorists. They were accused of tyranny and terrorism. Politicians demanded that their pensions be cut off and that they be excluded from society, and this happened more and more, until finally they were even forbidden to enter stores. Graffiti on walls of big cities even read, "Gas the unvaccinated" – a dreadful call against the backdrop of the German Holocaust. All this culminated in the statement of German Chancellor Olaf Scholz that for him there are "no more red lines" (*i.e.*, in the war against the "unvaccinated"). I don't know that a German chancellor has ever issued such a threat against a part of his own population – at least not after 1945. And all of a sudden, all those in authority at the federal and state levels announced the implementation of vaccine mandates for the entire German population, even though days earlier they had claimed that no one had any intention of doing so. And, in fact, vaccine mandates were introduced, at least for certain state employees (*e.g.*, in the military) and employees in certain institutions in the health and care sector (employees of hospitals, nursing homes, etc.) The fear among the people who refused the shot for various reasons was literally palpable, and quite a few of them thought about fleeing the country.

In this situation, my co-pastor Peter Schild and I felt compelled to pastorally assist our afflicted brothers and sisters, who often could not hope for any understanding from their churches, and therefore published on December 3, 2021, a "Counsel Regarding a Biblical Approach to the Covid Vaccination" (Part 3 of this book) seeking to address the fears and questions of the brothers and sisters and to encourage them to persevere in hope.

In the same month, together with other pastors and brothers, we founded the "Christian Corona Help Working Group" and called Christians nationwide to repentance and prayer. In addition, I penned the letter "Mandatory Vaccination and the Christian Conscience" (Part 4 of this book), which was sent on behalf of the Working Group and other Christian leaders on February 25, 2022, to those in authority at the federal and state levels and to all members of the German federal parliament, to explain to them the situation of many Christians and to appeal to them, in a clear but respectful manner, to refrain from introducing vaccine mandates.

On August 28, 2022, we held a conference on Covid. My lecture "Looking back on two years of Covid" (Part 5 of this book), in which I summarized the events, put them in a spiritual context and asked what lessons we should learn from the Covid era, provoked very controversial reactions, especially on the part of such pastors who felt (rightly or wrongly) criticized by the lecture. As with the sermon on Romans 13, I have deliberately refrained from adapting the wording of the lecture too much, in order to preserve its character.

At the conference, I also presented to the public a declaration on which I had been working since the spring of 2021 together with Dr. Paul Hartwig, pastor of Lakeside Chapel Betty's Bay, South Africa, and Steven Lloyd, pastor of *l'Église Protestante Évangélique du Narbonnais*, Narbonne, France, and which seeks to address the state measures from a biblical perspective: the "Frankfurt

Declaration of Christian and Civil Liberties" (Part 6 of this book). I myself was surprised at how positively the Frankfurt Declaration was received. Almost every brother to whom I sent the declaration in advance was willing to endorse it as an initial signatory, including Dr. John MacArthur, Dr. James White, Dr. Voddie Baucham, Dr. Joe Boot, Douglas Wilson, Dr. James Coates, Justin Peters, to name but a few. At the time of writing this foreword, more than 6,000 Christians from around the world have signed the Frankfurt Declaration.

A few days after the Frankfurt Declaration was presented, Ben Zeisloft published in *The Daily Wire* on September 6, 2022, the article "'Christians Against The Abuse Of Power': Theologians Around The World Sign Statement Rejecting Government Lockdowns" (Part 7 of this book), which is reprinted in this book by kind permission of *The Daily Wire*. The article is particularly interesting because Ben Zeisloft had asked five initial signers of the Frankfurt Declaration, namely Dr. Joe Boot, Dr. James White, Tim Stephens, Dr. John MacArthur, and myself, to each write a few explanatory thoughts on each of the five articles of the Frankfurt Declaration.

I was particularly pleased that Dr. John MacArthur, pastor of Grace Community Church, Sun Valley, California, USA, also published his own article one day later, on September 7, 2022, in which he explained in more detail the reasons for his support of the Frankfurt Declaration. The article "Why I Signed the Frankfurt Declaration" (Part 8 of this book) is also reprinted in this book with the kind permission of Dr. MacArthur.

As the Frankfurt Declaration gained international attention, I was asked by the English newspaper *Evangelical Times* to write an article on why I think the Frankfurt Declaration is necessary. The article was first published in the *Evangelical Times* on October 17, 2022, and was also published by *G3 Ministries* in the USA and by *Caldron Pool* in Australia in November 2022. In this book, the article "Why the Frankfurt Declaration is Necessary" (Part 9 of this book) is included.

Just before finishing this book, Jacob Reaume, the pastor of Trinity Bible Chapel in Waterloo, ON, Canada, sent me a very readable article he had just published. In this article titled "(How to) Love your Neighbor – The BioLogos Statement vs. The Frankfurt Declaration: Two Opposite Evangelical Responses to the State's Power" (Part 10 of this book), which was first published by *Christ Over All* on February 17, 2023, Pastor Reaume contrasts the BioLogos Statement, which affirms the Covid state measures, with the Frankfurt Declaration and convincingly demonstrates that the way professing Christians respond to Covid and state intervention is a matter of (good or bad) theology. The article is reprinted in this book with the kind permission of Pastor Reaume.

The last contribution in this book is a short address (Part 11 of this book) which I delivered on November 17, 2022, at the "Church At War" conference in Waterloo, Ontario, Canada. This conference brought together Canadian pastors who had steadfastly resisted government injustice during the Covid era and had been honored by being allowed to suffer for the Lord, partly through imprisonment, partly through fines amounting to millions of dollars, partly through excommunication by their own denomination. These include Dr. James Coates, Tim Stephens, Jacob Reaume, Dr. Aaron Rock, and Steve Richardson, among others. The like-mindedness among the brothers and the spiritual unity in the evaluation of the Covid events was a great encouragement for me, such as I hardly found among spiritual leaders in Germany. I want to include my address there in this book, to honor the influence of these Canadian pastors; for it was their courage and faithfulness, in the face of persecution, that encouraged me to speak out publicly.

It is my hope that the pieces collected in this book may inspire Christians who believed the narratives of the state in the Covid era, and submitted to its unjust orders, to reconsider and encourage them to be faithful and steadfast, lest they give to Caesar what is God's in future encroachments of the state. Moreover, I hope that this book will serve as a contemporary witness that there was resistance on the part of the church of Christ against the injustice of the Covid era, even if it had been limited to relatively few.

Finally, I would like to take this opportunity to first thank my beloved wife, Nicole. My public stance, during the Corona era, came with many fears and attacks, often from false brothers, but sometimes even from brothers from whom I would not have expected it. This did not remain without effect on my state of mind, at times. My wife was always at my side, during this time, and bore everything with me. I would also like to thank my co-pastor, Peter Schild, who not only courageously and steadfastly walked every step of the way with me, but who was also often challenged as my shepherd in these difficult times, showing much patience and understanding and always pointing me to Christ. Finally, my thanks go to my church. Even when attacks came from many sides, I could always be assured of their love and support.

In the end, however, my thanks go above all to my God, who has strengthened and sustained me through countless mercies and even used brothers from distant countries, such as the USA or

Canada, to encourage His unworthy servant. May His Kingdom unfold until it fills the whole earth! To Him, my Lord and God, Jesus Christ, the King of kings and Lord of lords, be honor and eternal dominion!

– Tobias Riemenschneider
February 2023

– Part 1 –

Keeping Jesus in the Center – Precisely Because of Corona

Biblical Refutation of the Thesis Paper "Keeping Jesus at the Center - Despite Corona"
Tobias Riemenschneider and Peter Schild

With this statement we oppose the thesis paper "Keeping Jesus in the Center – Despite Corona" by Michael Kotsch, Wilfried Plock, Matthias Swart, Marco Vedder and others, which was published in the current, second version on November 25, 2020, but only recently came to our attention. Since the thesis paper has a large number of theological deficiencies, we fear that biblical truths will be obscured by it and, thus, the consciences of some Christians will be grieved. We therefore see it as our duty to counter the most serious theological misconceptions of the thesis paper with a biblical view. In response to the theses stated in the thesis paper, we put forward the following antitheses:

1. It is the sacred duty of the church to name the wrongs in the state, expose the sins of those in authority and call them to repentance from their evil deeds.
2. Certain state-mandated Corona restrictions on churches violate God's commandments and the consciences of

many Christians, as the state improperly encroaches on Christ's lordship over the church.
3. All Christians are therefore called to obey God rather than men and to resist[1] unrighteousness in a godly manner, even if this may result in persecution by the state.

In the following, we will provide biblical evidence for these antitheses.

1. The Sacred Duty of the Church

The signatories of the thesis paper rightly point out (para. 2) that the church and the state are two separate spheres of God's authority. However, they fail to recognize the scope and limits of these spheres of authority. Thus, they obviously believe that the church should largely stay out of politics, *i.e.*, the affairs of the state. The thesis paper states in this regard that pastors "should not engage in party politics" and that ethically wrong or questionable laws of the state, but which leave the Christian the option of acting righteously, need not be opposed; the Bible nowhere declared it our duty to control the government or to resist questionable decisions.

In doing so, the signatories fail to recognize the sacred duty of the church to proclaim the Word of God to all people. Such proclamation includes pointing out wrongdoing, convicting of sin, and calling all people, including those in authority, to

---

[1] By resist, resistance, etc., we, throughout this statement, always mean resistance in the biblical sense, i.e., nonviolent through prayer, preaching, petitions and calls to repentance to politicians, taking legal action, or peaceful civil disobedience.

repent of their evil works and to obey God's commandments (Matt. 28:19, 20; Acts 17:30). As Christians, we must not take part in the unfruitful works of darkness, but rather expose them (Eph. 5:11). The weapon for this fight against darkness and wickedness, which is the word of God (Eph. 6:17), was not given by the Lord to His church in vain.

Throughout history, those who proclaimed the word of God have carried out this sacred duty: the prophet Nathan confronted King David for his adultery with Bathsheba and the murder of Uriah; the prophet Elijah confronted King Ahab for his idolatry and the confiscation of Naboth's vineyard; and the prophet John the Baptist confronted King Herod not only for his lawless marriage but for all the evil he had done, to name but a few examples. To the prophet Isaiah, the LORD commands, "Cry aloud; do not hold back; lift up your voice like a trumpet; declare to my people their transgression, to the house of Jacob their sins" (Isa 58:1). Even to heathen nations and kings, the prophets proclaimed judgment on their evil deeds. Thus, Daniel exhorted King Nebuchadnezzar, "Therefore, O king, let my counsel be acceptable to you: break off your sins by practicing righteousness, and your iniquities by showing mercy to the oppressed, that there may perhaps be a lengthening of your prosperity" (Dan. 4:27).

Today, the mission of the Church is to go and make disciples of all nations, baptizing them and teaching them to observe all that Christ has commanded us (Matt. 28:19, 20). This includes commanding all people everywhere to repent (Acts 17:30). This includes those who govern. Thus, the apostle Paul also preached righteousness and self-control and the coming judgment to Felix the governor (Acts 24:24,25).

When the apostle Paul writes that the state is a servant of

God, that is to praise the one who does good and to punish the one who does wrong, thus carrying out God's wrath (Rom. 13:3-6), it is essential to proclaim also to the public servants what God – their Lord, whom they are to serve – requires of them and what is good and to be praised, or wrong and to be punished, in His eyes. But who should make known to the rulers the will of God in regard to their exercise of authority, if not the church, to which the word of God has been entrusted, which is the pillar and buttress of the truth (1 Tim. 3:15)? Moreover, we are commanded to honor those in authority. Is it reverence if we let the rulers go to ruin without warning them that they are storing up for themselves the wrath of God through their unfaithful conduct in office?

Therefore, the church is not only permitted, but has a sacred duty to expose unrighteousness and wickedness on the part of those in authority as sin and – with the necessary reverence (Acts 23:3-5) – to call them to repentance when they do not live up to their task as God's servant but rebel against God, for instance – to take up an example from the thesis paper – by adopting so-called gay "marriage." The church must not remain silent on this! Speaking out against unrighteousness has nothing to do with "political party campaigning," but with fear of God and love of neighbor. Indeed, we must ask ourselves whether the current circumstances and the rampant lawlessness in politics are not also coming upon us because the church has been silent for too long about the wickedness and atrocities of the state.

The claim that "ethically wrong or questionable laws, but which leave the Christian the possibility to act righteously" do not have to be opposed seems naïve to us. The signatories themselves cite the example of gay "marriage." Do they not recognize the spirit behind such laws and that it does not settle for gay "marriage?" Have they not heard what these developments have already led to in other countries, where our brothers and sisters are prosecuted, for example, because a Christian baker refuses to bake a cake for such a "wedding," or a Christian registrar refuses to issue marriage certificates for such "marriages?" Many other examples could be listed.

2. The Present Injustice

The signatories of the thesis paper are of the opinion that certain state Corona restrictions for churches are to be observed by them. They justify this in two ways: on the one hand, the enactment of such measures would fall within the sphere of authority of the state, and on the other hand, the measures would not conflict with God's commandments. Both arguments are flawed.

On the one hand, the signatories claim (para. 3) that the only limitation to obedience to the state is "direct conflict" with a "clear command" of the word of God. Resistance to the state is "primarily about inalienable matters of faith." Unfortunately, it remains unclear what exactly the signatories mean by these terms, which in any case are not found in the Bible. Is it permissible to "indirectly" violate God's Word? Which requirements of God's Word are "unclear" and therefore need not be followed? And which matters of faith do the signatories regard as "alienable?" In any case, we would like to state that, for us, there are no alienable matters of faith, and would expect every Bible-believing Christian to agree with this.

The signatories then conclude that the Corona requirements for churches (*e.g.*, mask mandates, social distancing, limitations on the number of attendees) were subordinate issues; such "temporary regulations on external conditions and forms of church events" would not fundamentally violate biblical commands. Even though it is a thesis paper, it is nevertheless very astonishing that the signatories do not even begin to try to substantiate this all-decisive thesis biblically.

It is incomprehensible to us how one cannot recognize the spiritual dimension of the measures and dismiss them as mere externals. Do the signatories not see that the great distress of conscience of many God-fearing Christians and the "considerable tensions in the churches" are not simply caused by "temporary" (in some cases already lasting a year!) interferences in the merely "external conditions and forms of church meetings?" Rather, this distress of conscience arises from the fact that these measures are very much a violation of God's commandments. That the signatories do not recognize this is due to their misconception that they were not violating a "clear commandment" of the word of God. What they probably actually mean by this is a violation of an "explicit" commandment, for Scripture is never "unclear." Thus, unless Scripture contained the explicit commandment "Thou shalt worship on Sunday in person with the whole assembled congregation, without masks and without social distancing," there would not be a "clear commandment" of the word of God.

Such an approach to the word of God is without understanding. For not only explicit but also implicit commandments of the word of God are binding for Christians. Does not our Lord himself teach us this when He explains that the explicit commandment "You shall not murder" also includes the implicit commandment "You shall not be angry with your brother" or the explicit commandment "You shall not commit adultery" also includes the implicit commandment "You shall not look at a woman with lustful intent?"

The signatories' view that limitations on the number of attendees would not violate biblical commands reveals a deficient understanding of the church. The church is the body of Christ, and every member of the church is a member of that body. The gathering for worship is the gathering of the whole body, not just some parts of the body. Scripture gives explicit commands not to neglect to meet together (Heb. 10:25). (A livestream is neither a gathering nor a meeting). It is hard to estimate what spiritual harm churches have already suffered – and will continue to suffer – that have not gathered as a whole church for a year now and no longer celebrate the Lord's Supper together, which is supposed to serve to strengthen the whole body of Christ.

Moreover, limitations on the number of attendees impair the proclamation of the Word. For it is not only an impairment if the content of the proclamation is restricted, but also if the number of possible listeners is restricted. And aren't limitations on the number of attendees gross lack of love for those for whom there is no more room and who therefore have to stay at home? How dare the state presume to determine how many people may gather to worship God, the Creator of heaven and earth? Is this really a "subordinate" issue?

It is certainly not a subordinate issue for Dr. James Coates, pastor of GraceLife Church of Edmonton, Canada. Pastor Coates understands that the limitations on the number of attendees do indeed violate God's commandments, and he held services with the entire church despite threats from the authorities. For his courageous faithfulness to the word of God, this husband and father is now in prison. When Satan tempted him there and he was offered that he could be released immediately if he would only promise to comply with the Corona restrictions, he refused. His wife understands that her husband is doing this out of love for his Lord and Savior, and commented on her husband's decision to remain in prison, saying, "I love him for that." May the Lord reward our brother James Coates and his family! If the signers of the thesis paper are consistent, they must argue that the state was justified in taking action against Pastor Coates because he was guilty of sinfully resisting the state, even though the state's measures did not violate biblical commands. Do the signers really want to go down this road?

It is astonishing that the signatories do not even mention the state ban on congregational singing, which had already been in force for more than half a year in some German states at the time of the publication of the thesis paper. Does this prohibition not fit the thrust of the thesis paper, because here it obviously cannot be denied that Scripture is full of "clear" commands concerning singing (*cf.* for instance Ps. 47:7)? In the view of the signatories, would resistance be called for here? For what authority does the state have to deny the LORD His praises to be sung to Him? Singing is an inalienable element of biblical worship.

But also mask mandates and social distancing requirements for worship can violate the consciences of Christians. Are we not called to greet one another with the holy kiss (Rom. 16:16; 1 Cor. 16:20; 2 Cor. 13:12; 1 Thes. 5:26; 1 Peter 5:14) and to express brotherly love for one another? Of course, you can keep your distance for a while when you are sick so as not to infect anyone. But state-imposed masked distance for months and possibly years? It is baffling to us how one cannot recognize that this causes significant spiritual and psychological harm. After all, the signatories themselves write that they are confronted with major pastoral challenges. We can well relate to this, because we have cried with those who suffer from loneliness and alienation, or who despair because their church has been gathering for a year only with social distancing and masks, or not at all. Does this not violate the commandment to love one another and have heartfelt compassion for one another?

And what if someone's conscience is violated when he is made to meet his God and his brothers and sisters only masked, for months and perhaps years – actually something that naturally triggers distrust, unease and fear in us? What if he considers it unloving to give his brothers and sisters the impression, through distancing and masking, that he considers them a danger to life and limb from which he must protect himself? What if his fear of God forbids him to worship his Lord with his face covered? Are these not understandable reasons why a Christian may be compelled by his conscience to oppose these measures? Would it not be sinful for him to comply with them nonetheless? Therefore, it is wrong for pastors to make compliance with the commandments of men a condition for participation in worship, thereby domineering over the consciences of their sheep.

On the other hand, the signatories claim (para. 2) that the state regulations also apply to the congregation and that the state's sphere of control only ends where the interpretation of the Bible or the spiritual and ethical areas of congregational life are concerned; in all "external" aspects, the congregations would have to bow to state rules; the thesis paper gives some examples of this (building law, labor law, safety, finance law, criminal law).

As already stated above, it is incomprehensible to us how the signatories cannot recognize the spiritual and ethical dimension of the Covid restrictions and be of the opinion that these are simply external aspects, comparable, for example, to building law. We are not aware that Christians have ever had conflicts of conscience because of state requirements to build an emergency exit or install a fire extinguisher.

The reason for this is that the examples cited in the thesis do not directly concern the circumstances of worship, for in such matters the state has no God-given authority. Otherwise, the state could far too easily hinder the practice of faith by, for example, permanently limiting the number of attendees for religious services to ten people. But then the state would not be acting within its sphere of authority, but as a tyrant. This must be resisted!

Once the state has invaded the sphere of authority of the church, how do we know that it will not, step by step, extend its dominion further and further and impose more and more restrictions on churches? We are alarmed at how readily churches give up their freedoms, for which our brothers and sisters have fought, suffered, and in some cases laid down their lives in past centuries. It is precisely because we take seriously the Bible's command to love our neighbor and love our children and grandchildren that we jealously guard the freedoms of the church and of our neighbor.

We are particularly surprised that some Christians even think they have to be grateful to the state for "allowing" church services at all. In a reader comment on the thesis paper, for example, it says, "Full agreement! The state also grants the church (...) many privileges (...) even under the current measures." Such statements reveal a fundamentally erroneous understanding of the state, which, although not explicitly advocated in the thesis paper, is nevertheless promoted by it. It is not the state that graciously allows us to worship (under many restrictions), but this is our God-given right. The state, as God's servant, is obligated to ensure the undisturbed exercise of this right. We should not thank the state for "allowing" us to worship, but the state should be afraid to interfere with the worship of God. Our thanks are due to God alone for still restraining our state so that it cannot persecute the church as it does elsewhere.

However, one could now object that in the event of a present danger to life and limb, Christians may very well modify certain aspects of the worship service in order to protect themselves and others. The Covid measures must therefore also be evaluated against the background of the actual epidemiological situation and the question answered as to whether, at present, attending a church service without limiting the number of participants, keeping distance and wearing a mask poses a real and present danger to those attending the service.

In this regard, the signatories claim (para. 5) that the situation was obscure. Therefore, Christians would be allowed to decide which physicians or politicians they trust and should display an attitude of humility and readiness to be corrected. We do not believe that this assessment of the situation honors the truth. We understand when the situation may seem confusing to individual Christians, especially when they are exposed to the influence of certain media, or the ungodly, and cannot find a counterbalance to this in the church. But it is the duty of pastors to inform themselves comprehensively and to assess the situation on the basis of the knowledge they have gained in order to lead their sheep rightly. Ignorance is not virtuous humility, but folly.

At the time of publication of the thesis paper, numerous scientific studies, figures and facts from all over the world were available, which allowed a very realistic assessment of both the danger of the coronavirus and the effectiveness and suitability of the state measures. We encourage readers to critically inform themselves about this. Precisely because the situation was no longer obscure, but was now easy to assess, Dr. John MacArthur, pastor of Grace Community Church in Los Angeles, USA, began in July 2020, in defiance of California state regulations and under threat of imprisonment, to hold services with the entire church again – and for this he was publicly criticized by some of the signatories of the thesis paper.

Notably, co-initiator Michael Kotsch has accused Dr. MacArthur of dishonest motives for his decision, claiming in a video on his YouTube channel that Dr. MacArthur "may (...) be far less concerned with Jesus' commands than with Grace Community Church's business model," adding that Dr. MacArthur had also, in the past, "reinterpreted clear biblical statements" "because they did not fit the interests of his ministry."[2] Since we do not assume that Mr. Kotsch has the gift to fathom the thoughts and dispositions of Dr. MacArthur's heart, we hereby publicly rebuke him for this publicly committed sin of slander. "Who are you to pass judgment on the servant of another?" (Rom. 14:4).

Regardless of how one assesses the present situation, decisions on measures relating to worship must always weigh the risks to life and limb against the risks to soul and spirit – however, the state is not qualified to make such an assessment, since it cannot understand and judge spiritual matters. Pastors must keep in mind that they are to keep watch over the souls of their sheep as those who will have to give an account (Heb. 13:17).

---

2 Michael Kotsch. "John MacArthur Irrt! (Von Michael Kotsch)," September 9, 2020. https://www.youtube.com/watch?v=-FefSVNgIpg.

We also find it incomprehensible that the thesis paper states that Christians would be allowed to decide which politicians they "trust." Should Christians really trust ungodly politicians and not rather critically examine their statements to determine whether they correspond to the truth? Have the signers not understood that every person's thoughts and actions are marked by spiritual influences, either the Spirit of truth or the spirit of error (1 John 4:6)? That one is either with Christ or against Him (Luke 11:23)? That there are only two kinds of people in this world, believers and unbelievers (2 Cor. 6:15), light and darkness (2 Cor. 6:14), the children of God and the children of the devil (1 John 3:10)?

Have the signers not read how our Lord speaks that the children of the devil want to do their father's desires, who is a murderer and the father of lies (John 8:44)? Is this not true of the politicians who validate the murder of 100,000 unborn children a year in our country, calling it "reproductive health/justice," denying the truth about the nature of marriage, family, gender, sexuality, indeed, denying their Creator Himself?

God has given the state the responsibility, as His servant, to commend the one who does what is good and to punish the one who does wrong (Rom. 13:3-6). Is it not obvious that the state is fulfilling this responsibility less and less and that this development has accelerated drastically, especially in the last few months? That the state increasingly calls evil good and good evil (Isa. 5:20)? For example, on the same day that the current version of the thesis paper was published, November 25, 2020, our brother Pastor Olaf Latzel was convicted by the state of incitement of the people for proclaiming biblical truths.

Doesn't the current crisis also show that those in authority are not afraid to adopt measures that are obviously evil, even depriving us of rights that all human beings have as creatures made in the image of God? For example, when they prohibit countless people from working for months, even though God commands that man should work and provide for his family? When people are punished for visiting and holding family members, celebrating their wedding, or saying goodbye to a loved one at their funeral? When a father is prohibited from being present at the birth of his child or a daughter is prohibited from holding the hand of her dying mother? Many other examples could be given. Especially when politicians claim that all this is necessary for our protection, we should remember the words of our Lord, "The kings of the Gentiles exercise lordship over them, and those in authority over them are called benefactors" (Luke 22:25).

But how should we deal with the anxious brothers and sisters who, according to the thesis paper (para. 6), should be especially accommodated in the Covid period? Should we perhaps comply with the measures out of love and consideration for them?

The signatories themselves acknowledge (para. 1) that people ultimately do not die from an illness or accident, but from the will or permission of God. The Bible even teaches that the LORD has determined from the beginning on which day we will die (Ps. 139:16). And our Lord asks the rhetorical question, "And which of you by being anxious can add a single hour to his span of life?" (Matt. 6:27; Luke 12:25). Does not our Lord exhort us again and again not to fear, even death? Is not dying our gain, and should we not desire to depart and be with Christ (Phil. 1:21, 23)? Has not Christ delivered all of us who through fear of death were subject to lifelong slavery (Heb. 2:15)?

Certainly, a Christian can be afraid of sickness or death, and we are not to tempt the Lord our God recklessly. But we must not live in a state of constant fear and neglect even the commandments of God out of anxiety for our lives. So how do we rightly respond to anxious brothers and sisters? How do we love them as brothers? By accepting and affirming their fear, which is ultimately an expression of their little faith? Or by helping them to overcome their anxiety through the truth and faith?

3. Call to Faithfulness

The signatories should examine themselves to see if their worldview is really determined by the Bible alone or rather by worldly, secular thinking and pragmatism - lest they incur persecution by the state. Yet does not the apostle Paul write, "Indeed, all who desire to live a godly life in Christ Jesus will be persecuted?" (2 Tim. 3:12). If we always submit to the state and compromise over one thing after another, we will probably avoid persecution, but our witness for Christ Jesus will suffer.

We are particularly appalled by the fact that some of the signers of the thesis paper, in other publications, publicly rebuke such Christians who are convicted by the word of God and their conscience of having to resist the state, and in some cases accuse them of evil intentions. We hereby make it known that in this regard we stand firmly with our beloved brethren John MacArthur and James Coates, and all those who are persecuted for their godliness. We urge the undersigned to think carefully about which side they wish to take.

We exhort all Christians not to be caught up in the madness that has taken hold of the whole world and enslaves people in a constant fear of death, but to courageously put their hope in

Christ, who is the Life. Let us be a witness in this dark time by loving the truth and meeting in cordial brotherly love! Let us reform all our thinking by the word of God, that we may gain a biblical worldview by taking every thought captive to obey Christ (2 Cor. 10:5). "Do not be conformed to this world, but be transformed by the renewal of your mind, that by testing you may discern what is the will of God, what is good and acceptable and perfect" (Rom. 12:2). Let us pray for those who suffer affliction or persecution for the sake of the Word, that they may endure to the end! Every Christian should consider how he can help such through letters, donations, or writing to politicians!

Finally, we call on all pastors to carry out their sacred duty and preach courageously against the wrongs and sins of those in authority, and also to respectfully call them to repentance, either verbally or in writing! We exhort pastors and churches to no longer withhold honor from God and burden the consciences of Christians with commandments of men, but to once again worship as God commands: with the gathered congregation, in biblically commanded brotherly meeting, and with joyful singing of praise to the glory of the LORD!

Render unto Caesar the things that are Caesar's, but render unto God the things that are God's. And if Caesar persecutes us for it, let us suffer it with joy. Let us be encouraged, brothers and sisters, to faithfully follow our Lord in these times, as He says, "Do not fear what you are about to suffer. Behold, the devil is about to throw some of you into prison, that you may be tested, and for ten days you will have tribulation. Be faithful unto death, and I will give you the crown of life" (Rev. 2:10). To conclude with the words of the thesis paper, "Too much is at stake."

– Part 2 –

Submission and Resistance
Tobias Riemenschneider

Sermon Text: Romans 13:1-7

Let every person be subject to the governing authorities. For there is no authority except from God, and those that exist have been instituted by God. Therefore, whoever resists the authorities resists what God has appointed, and those who resist will incur judgment. For rulers are not a terror to good conduct, but to bad. Would you have no fear of the one who is in authority? Then do what is good, and you will receive his approval, for he is God's servant for your good. But if you do wrong, be afraid, for he does not bear the sword in vain. For he is the servant of God, an avenger who carries out God's wrath on the wrongdoer. Therefore, one must be in subjection, not only to avoid God's wrath but also for the sake of conscience. For because of this you also pay taxes, for the authorities are ministers of God, attending to this very thing. Pay to all what is owed to them: taxes to whom taxes are owed, revenue to whom revenue is owed, respect to whom respect is owed, honor to whom honor is owed.

Introduction

The topic we are dealing with today did not really play a role in our Western world for many decades. In other countries of the world, however, it did. Just ask our brothers and sisters from the former USSR. But in our "Christian West," which was characterized by Christian thinking and Christian values, the question of the relationship between state and church or state and Christian was basically settled. The constitutions of the states of the Western world contain certain fundamental rights, including freedom of religion. For example, the German Constitution states in Art. 4, "Freedom of faith and of conscience and freedom to profess a religious or philosophical creed shall be inviolable," and, "The undisturbed practice of religion shall be guaranteed." In other words, you may believe what you want in our country, you may profess your faith as you want, and you may practice your faith as you want, and the state has to stay out of it. The state has no authority to interfere with citizens' faith or worship. And in order to ensure that the state cannot do this, the constitution includes the constitutional right to freedom of religion. For constitutional rights are the citizen's rights of defense against the state. So, if the state should encroach, the citizens can defend themselves by pointing out this constitutional right to the state and saying, "Stop! So far and no further!"

And for many decades, that worked quite well. But unfortunately, our constitution is just a piece of paper. What is decisive is not so much what is written on the paper, but how the rulers and judges interpret and apply it. Now, the problem is that our constitution comes from a Christian worldview and therefore only functions in a state that has some sort of Christian worldview.

And our state no longer has that; the de-Christianization in our state has progressed too far. One example: Article 6 of the German Constitution places marriage under the special protection of the state. For the fathers of the Constitution, it was clear what they meant by this. They had a Christian worldview and therefore it was clear to them: They wanted to protect and promote marriage between a man and a woman as the union from which children are born, the nucleus of society. But today, 70 years later, the rulers and judges in our country have a secular, godless, anti-Christian worldview. They deny that marriage is a creation order and that therefore God defines what marriage is. They believe marriage to be a social construct and defined by man. And if society changes, people could redefine marriage too. And so, in 2017, under a shower of confetti, the German rulers resolved that a marriage could also be between two men or two women or two "diverse," and the judges did not oppose this. And therefore, our Constitution now protects something it was never intended to protect, namely, not the union from which life springs, but a godless, sinful lifestyle. The text of the Constitution has not changed, but its interpretation and application have. And thus, the Constitution has been completely perverted and twisted. Marriage is no longer under the special protection of the state as something sacred, but has been made equal to an abomination.

You see, we often wonder when the judgment of God will come upon our godless country. The answer is, it is already here! We are witnessing the wrath of God being revealed against our country. Look at Romans 1: Our state denies God, it denies God in schools throughout the country. Our nation no longer has natural love, it even kills its own children by the masses. And claiming to be wise, people became fools. Isn't that what we're seeing everywhere right now? How people rely so much on their science and thereby make fools of themselves? And therefore, God has given our country up to all kinds of lusts and sins, and especially to the public and state-supported practice and endorsement of homosexuality. These are clear signs of judgment on our country. That doesn't mean it won't get worse. It will get worse, but the judgment has already begun.

I am telling you this because it is important that we understand that our Western world is undergoing a tremendous upheaval that is bringing about drastic changes. This upheaval began a long time ago, but now it is nearing completion. The foundations are being overturned. And therefore, we can no longer rely on the fact that our faith and worship will be protected in our states, even if it still says so on paper. The rulers will interfere with our faith and worship, and the judges will not protect us. We have known this for a long time. Those who saw the signs of the times knew that sooner or later the state would continue to encroach on other areas of life. Because if we preach biblical truths, for example about homosexuality or transsexuality or certain other things, then in the eyes of this state we are hate preachers who cannot be tolerated, but who must be dealt with, who must be muzzled. For them, it is vital to protect this new anti-Christian world from biblical Christianity. Not from the Christianity of the big churches – that conforms to the world – but from true, biblical Christianity.

We knew this was coming, but we thought we still had time. And then came 2020 and came the Covid crisis. And the state encroached on worship like it had never dared to do before. And on top of that, in this very year, the state actually dared, for the first time, to convict a pastor as an inciter of the people because of biblical statements on homosexuality: our beloved brother Pastor

Olaf Latzel. We are in the midst of God's judgment, in an anti-Christian world.

And suddenly the question of the relationship between state and church or state and Christian is red-hot, and it is extremely important that we deal with it. Because the current crisis has caught most churches completely unprepared, our church included. And it has been revealed in this crisis that many churches have major, serious theological deficiencies; deficiencies that call into question whether these churches can survive such a crisis at all, whether they can exist at all in this new de-Christianized world. Or whether these deficiencies will not lead to apostasy in the end. I will give a few examples.

Some Failures of the Modern Western Church

A deficient ecclesiology, *i.e.*, a deficient doctrine of the church, is evident. Worship services with only 30% of the brothers and sisters? No problem. Online services? A great thing, a wonderful advancement! There are churches that have not met for a year. To these churches I say, "By definition, you are no longer a church. For a church is the called-out, physically gathered body of Christ, gathered in heartfelt brotherly love, which also expresses itself in physical nearness."

A deficient understanding of Scripture is evident. "We must only do what is expressly written in the word of God. And as long as it doesn't explicitly state, 'Thou shalt gather physically in one place every Sunday as the whole church, with no social distancing and no masks,' then we have total freedom." That is never the way to deal with God's Word!

A deficient understanding of epistemology, that is, the doctrine of how we know whether something is true or not, is evident. And this is combined with a completely unbiblical worldview. It is foolish for Christians to believe that the state is somehow neutral and can surely be trusted. "The very state that denies basic truths about creation that every child understands, about male and female, marriage, family, sexuality, gender, yes, that denies the Creator Himself, it will surely not lie to us! The state, that is responsible for the murder of 100,000 children in the womb every year, it surely wants to protect our lives!" We Christians must be friends of truth, not of lies. Thomas Jefferson Franklin once said, "It is error alone which needs the support of government. Truth can stand by itself."

Associated with this is a poor knowledge of history. We all know very little about history, both church history and secular history. And because of that, some think the current situation is somehow similar to plagues from the past. So, pastors and professors quote Richard Baxter or Martin Luther and just apply that to our situation. And apart from the fact that these people misunderstand these two men of God even in their original context, these had to deal with the plague and the cholera at that time. Take a look at the history books. Then you will understand how Christians dealt with great diseases. They did not scatter and stop gathering; they did not keep their distance or wear masks. They held the dying in their arms! Then they became ill and died, and the next one held them in their arms. They had the right understanding of what life and death mean to a Christian.

A deficient understanding of persecution is also evident, again linked to a deficient knowledge of church history. The unspoken assumption is "Persecution is only if it is directed specifically and exclusively against Christians for being Christians." This is utter nonsense. If this was true, then there was very little persecution in the history of the church. Ironically, the very people who claim this will probably never be persecuted. Because you don't wait to be persecuted until you start keeping God's commandments, but you keep God's commandments and that is precisely why you will be persecuted. If the state mandates something that affects everyone, and everyone can comply with it, but you cannot comply with it for the sake of the word, because of your faith, and therefore the state punishes you, that is persecution. I'll say a little more about this later.

A lack of understanding of Christian unity is evident. Some accuse us of jeopardizing Christian unity with our stance. As if Christian unity consisted of simply keeping one's mouth shut and not talking about controversial issues! Christian unity is not simply a hypocritical outward unity, but being of one mind. Should we not be allowed to have public debate on theological disputes because of the mere outward pretense of unity? Then half of church history, including the Reformation, would not have happened.

A lack of understanding of the testimony of Christians in this world is also evident. Some really think that our testimony would be to please men, so no one would get angry with us and consider us irresponsible. Our true testimony is faithfulness to our Lord and His commandments, and the world will hate us for it! This is our testimony as Christians.

Much more could be said, but lastly: a crisis of leadership is evident. Because the pastors who are supposed to be courageous and strong and manly, especially in times like these, are often the ones saying all this nonsense and tormenting their sheep with it, and I'm afraid many of them do so primarily because they don't want to be persecuted.

And because in the future a true church will increasingly be discerned from an apostate church by whether it understands when to submit to the state and when to resist it, and whether it is willing to suffer persecution for the sake of the Word, it is so important that we have a theology firmly grounded in Scripture about these things. And here, too, we have examples from the USSR. The brothers and sisters there judged by precisely such things whether a church had fallen away: whether or not it had registered with the state and submitted to it. That is why we need a theology about these things that is grounded in Scripture.

And that is my goal: to lay such a foundation. So, let's approach the key text on this subject in two points: (1) submission to the state; and (2) resistance to the state.

1. Submission to the State

Let every person be subject to the governing authorities. Each of us must be subject to the governing authorities. The Greek word translated as "subject to" comes from military language and means to take the place under the commander assigned to you. So, we are to take the place assigned to us, and that place is under the governing authorities. And we take this place not only outwardly and reluctantly, but inwardly and willingly.

And we are subject to the *governing authorities*. Plural. We are subject to all governing authorities. So, we are not only subject to the police standing in front of us with drawn gun, but to all governing authorities, from the President down to the lowest clerk of a government agency. To be subject to the governing authorities means: (1) we acknowledge that they are above us and do not treat them disrespectfully or demandingly, but (2) we treat them with reverence; and (3) we obey them – subject to certain limitations; more on that later. So, the next time a deputy writes you a ticket for parking, you don't snap at him, but you apologize for your lack of submission and respectfully thank him for his service. And when the state puts up signs saying you can drive 60 mph, you don't drive 90 mph, you drive 60 mph. And you do it gladly. You see, this is a very serious issue. As Christians, we must be subject to the state.

However, this submission only applies to the authorities who are actually above us in a certain area. The deputy can write you a ticket. But if he stands at your door the next day and wants to search your home, he has no authority to do so – at least not without a warrant. In this area, he is not above you, and you do not have to be subject to him. Yes, on the contrary, it would be foolish for you to let him in. We will take up this thought again later.

But why should we be subject to the governmental authorities? Are we afraid of man? Do we submit because they are stronger or smarter or wiser? No, the reason is another. Continuing verse 1, *For there is no authority except from God, and those that exist have been instituted by God.* So why should we be subject to the governmental authorities? Paul gives two reasons: first and general: because every authority comes from God; and second and particular: because the existing authorities have been instituted by God.

All authority comes from God. Only God has authority in Himself, and He has all authority; He *is* the blessed and only Sovereign. And if any man has any authority, it is only because God gave it to him. We read this very fundamentally in the creation account in Genesis 1:27-28,

> So God created man in his own image, in the image of God he created him; male and female he created them. And God blessed them. And God said to them, 'Be fruitful and multiply and fill the earth and subdue it, and have dominion over the fish of the sea and over the birds of the heavens and over every living thing that moves on the earth.'"

It is God who gives dominion to men. God created all men equal in His image. There is no human being who is above another human being *per se*. If anyone has authority, it comes from God: if the parents have authority over the children, the husband over the wife, the pastors over the sheep, the employer over the employee, the state over the citizen – everyone has his authority from God.

But since all authority is delegated by God, this also means that everyone who is in authority is only a steward of that authority, which actually is God's, and that he will one day have to answer to God for how he has handled the authority delegated to him. God will demand an account from everyone to whom He delegates authority, including the rulers. And that is why God also gives instructions in Scripture on the character that a ruler must possess to be able to carry out his duties properly: He is to be diligent, godly, trustworthy, hating unjust gain. And he shall have a copy of the Scripture with him, as it is written in Deuteronomy 17:19-20,

> And it shall be with him, and he shall read in it all the days of

his life, that he may learn to fear the Lord his God by keeping all the words of this law and these statutes, and doing them, that his heart may not be lifted up above his brothers, and that he may not turn aside from the commandment, either to the right hand or to the left.

This is what a ruler must be according to the will of God. You see, that is why the church must also preach to those in authority, convicting them of their sins and proclaiming to them that they are God's servants and what it is that God requires of them, what is good and evil according to His standard. Who else should do this if not us, who are entrusted with the oracles of God?

Every authority is delegated by God, and God will demand an account from the rulers as to how they have used that authority. People tend to forget this and like to think they have authority themselves, and so occasionally they need to be reminded that they are mistaken. This is what Jesus did to Pilate in John 19:10-11, "So Pilate said to him, 'You will not speak to me? Do you not know that I have authority to release you and authority to crucify you?' Jesus answered him, 'You would have no authority over me at all unless it had been given you from above.'" Every authority comes from God. And not only is every authority from God in general, but the existing governmental authorities are also decreed by God in a very concrete way. In Dan. 2:21 it says about God, "He changes times and seasons; he removes kings and sets up kings." God has decreed that there be a king, and He has decreed who that king is. And this is true not only for kings, but for everyone in authority: for governors all the way down to the lowest governmental authority. For Germany, God has decreed that there be a Chancellor, and He has set up Mrs. Merkel in that office. He has decreed that there be a Minister of Health, and he has set up Mr. Spahn in that office. He has decreed that there be a governor of the state of Hesse, and he has set up Mr. Bouffier in that office, and so on, all the way down to the lowest public servant. This does not mean that every ruler is pleasing to God. God has set up many ungodly, wicked kings. More on this later as well. First, let us note that all governmental authorities have been instituted by God.

And that is why verse 2 continues, *Therefore, whoever resists the authorities resists what God has appointed, and those who resist will incur judgment.* You want to resist the state? Beware! You don't simply resist men or human institutions, but you resist God Himself and what He has appointed. By the way, this is also not only true of governmental authorities, but everywhere someone has authority, because remember, all authority comes from God. Children who resist their parents resist God and His ordinances. Wives who resist their husbands, Christians who resist their pastors, employees who resist their employers, and citizens who resist the state all resist God and His ordinances.

And whoever resists God will be judged. Verse 2, *those who resist will incur judgment.* Why is that? Verses 3 and 4:

> *For rulers are not a terror to good conduct, but to bad. Would you have no fear of the one who is in authority? Then do what is good, and you will receive his approval, for he is God's servant for your good. But if you do wrong, be afraid, for he does not bear the sword in vain. For he is the servant of God, an avenger who carries out God's wrath on the wrongdoer.*

So why did God institute the governmental authorities? What

is the purpose of the governmental authorities and the rulers? Are they to protect us from each and every risk in life? No, but first, they are to be a terror to bad conduct by punishing the wrongdoer; and second, they are to be an incentive to good conduct by giving approval to one who does good. Thus, the state is to restrain evil and promote good.

And by doing these two things, the state is acting as God's servant. Whether the rulers know it or not, whether they want it or not, they are God's servants. When the state commends the one who does good, it is acting as God's servant; verse 3, *Would you have no fear of the one who is in authority? Then do what is good, and you will receive his approval, for he is God's servant for your good.* And when the state punishes the wrongdoer, it is acting as God's servant; verse 4, *But if you do wrong, be afraid, for he does not bear the sword in vain. For he is the servant of God, an avenger who carries out God's wrath on the wrongdoer.* When the state does these things, it is acting as God's servant because it is God's right to judge. He is the avenger and judge of the world, rewarding the righteous and punishing the unrighteous. He will do so ultimately on the Last Day, at the end of time, but He does it in part even now. He does it in various ways, through sickness and death, through calamities and catastrophes, through giving over to sin; and He does it by using the governmental authorities as His servant.

The state is given for good to him who does good, by commending him and guarding him from harm, by protecting his God-given rights and liberties from those who want to take our lives, our freedom, our property; and in this it acts as God's servant. And it is given as punishment to the wrongdoer, because it carries out God's wrath on the wrongdoer, and in this it also acts as God's servant. And for the carrying out of vengeance and wrath, God has given the state a special instrument, namely the sword, *for he does not bear the sword in vain.* The sword, not the prison keys! The sword is a tool for killing. Paul writes here that God has given the state the power to punish wrongdoers – even with capital punishment. In fact, this is the first commandment that God gives to mankind for a beginning state system, for a system of law enforcement. After the Fall and the expulsion from Paradise, men became more and more wicked until God put an end to their wrongdoing and destroyed the whole world in the Flood. And after the Flood, God begins to institute a system of law enforcement, to institute governmental authorities so that things would not grow as bad as they were before; and He gives a first commandment to this end. We read in Genesis 9:6, "Whoever sheds the blood of man, by man shall his blood be shed, for God made man in his own image."

God commanded the state to carry out capital punishment, and He empowered it to do so by giving it the sword; and He did not give it to it in vain. Therefore, if capital punishment has been abolished almost everywhere in the Western world after 4,500 years, it is not a sign of advancement but of falling away from God. The state no longer does what God gave to it as the first commandment in the very beginning. Being against capital punishment is not Christianity, but anti-Christian humanism.

And because the state is God's servant, commending good and punishing bad, no one who does good need be afraid of the state, for the state will give approval to him; and every wrongdoer should be afraid of the state, for the state will execute vengeance and wrath on him, and even with the sword. Verse 3, *Would you have no fear of the one who is in authority? Then do what is good, and you will receive his approval, for he is God's servant for your good. But if you do wrong, be afraid.* To all wrongdoers, the state should be a terror, for it will punish them, with death if necessary. But as Christians, whose mission in life is to do good, we should be able to rejoice in the state. We should praise and thank God for His good ordinance, for His servant, because it gives approval to us and protects us from the wrongdoer. If the state carries out its duty properly, then what we read in 2 Samuel 23:3-4 applies to it, "When one rules justly over men, ruling in the fear of God, he dawns on them like the morning light, like the sun shining forth on a cloudless morning, like rain that makes grass to sprout from the earth." This is how God intends the state to be: given for our good, for our blessing, for our joy. I don't know if this image comes to your mind when you think of Mrs. Merkel or others. But this is how God intended it to be.

And because the state, as God's servant, commends the one who does good and punishes the wrongdoer, we are to be subject to it. Why, exactly? Verse 5, *Therefore one must be in subjection, not only to avoid God's wrath but also for the sake of conscience.* We should be subject to the state because of wrath. You want to rebel against the state? The state will punish you, perhaps even with death. But we must be subject to the state not only because of fear of wrath, but also for the sake of conscience. Why for the sake of conscience? Well, the conscience distinguishes between good and wrong. And therefore, it tells you that it is good and right to be subject to the state, because the state promotes good and punishes wrong. You want to rebel against the state? You want to rebel against God's servant that commends the good and punishes the wrong? That is wicked! That goes against conscience. Therefore, you must not do that *for the sake of conscience.*

What should we do instead? From verse 6, *For because of this you also pay taxes, for the authorities are ministers of God, attending to this very thing. Pay to all what is owed to them: taxes to whom taxes are owed, revenue to whom revenue is owed, respect to whom respect is owed, honor to whom honor is owed.* Because rulers are God's servants, even God's ministers, and continually do this good service – that is their occupation, their job – therefore we also pay them for their service by paying taxes and paying revenue; and we show them respect by honoring them, precisely because they do a good service.

And in addition, it says in 1 Timothy 2:1-4,

> First of all, then, I urge that supplications, prayers, intercessions, and thanksgivings be made for all people, for kings and all who are in high positions, that we may lead a peaceful and quiet life, godly and dignified in every way. This is good, and it is pleasing in the sight of God our Savior, who desires all people to be saved and to come to the knowledge of the truth.

So, we pray and plead for the rulers. For among them, too, there are those whom God wants to save and lead to the knowledge of the truth. And we give thanks to God for the rulers. For He has set them up for our good. For if we had no state to punish the wrongdoers, we would have anarchy, and no one would restrain your wicked neighbor from taking your car, and taking your house, and taking your wife, and taking all that is yours, and beating you to death. It is a blessing and a cause for gratitude that God has ordained the state. This is the biblical theology of the Christian's submission to the state authorities.

But that is only half of the truth. And many Christians stop at this one half of the truth. This is why we receive comments in response to our statement "Keeping Jesus in the Center," accusing us of violating "the clear commandment of Romans 13." You see, it is a big problem of our time that many interpret the Bible so shallowly and, moreover, have no idea of church history. For this dispute is not new, but has been going on for 2,000 years, and faithful brothers have written whole books about it. In the time of the Reformation this was an important topic: the Magdeburg Confession, *Vindiciae contra tyrannos* by the Huguenots, *Lex Rex* by Samuel Rutherford. It was also an important topic in the Third Reich with the Barmen Declaration and the Confessing Church. And in these 2,000 years, this text has also been misused again and again by rulers and preachers to demand of Christians absolute submission to the state. A theologian once wrote that the misuse of Romans 13 has caused "more misfortune and misery than any other seven verses of the New Testament" – the misuse, that is, not the proper use. I quote from a call to disobey the state's Corona measures by Tim Cantrell, pastor of Antioch Bible Church in South Africa:

> In July 1933, during Hitler's first summer in power, a young German pastor named Joachim Hossenfelder preached a sermon in the towering Kaiser Wilhelm Memorial Church, Berlin's most important church. He used the words of Romans 13 to remind worshippers of the importance of obedience to those in authority. The church was all decked out with Nazi banners, its pews packed with the Nazi faithful and soldiers in uniform. Earlier that same year, Friedrich Dibelius, a German bishop and one of the highest Protestant officials in the country, had also preached on Romans 13 to justify all the

Nazi seizures of power and brutal policies, and misquoting Martin Luther himself about the supposed paramount powers of state authority. Three days after this sermon, the German parliament dissolved, and Hitler took over. Within a few years, six million Jews had been slaughtered and the world devastated by World War Two.

I am not saying that we are at the same point today as we were in 1933, but I want to warn those who think that Romans 13 demands absolute subjection to the state or allows resistance only if we are forbidden to speak of Jesus. Be careful not to join a very inglorious tradition of misuse of Romans 13! If only the churches had preached the truth back in 1933! Who knows what might have been prevented. But when is resistance to the state the right, or even the duty, of a Christian?

2. Resistance to the State

Most Christians agree that the Bible, including Romans 13, does not demand absolute subjection to the state, absolute obedience. Our subjection to the state is unconditional, but not unlimited. By this I mean that we are not subject to the state only when it meets our conditions. We do not say, "I will be subject to the state only when a Bible-believing Christian is Chancellor." No, we submit to the state even when it is godless. Our subjection is unconditional in this sense. But it is not unlimited. There are limits to our subjection. And indeed, those limits are found here in Romans 13. This may be surprising to some, because at first glance Romans 13 seems quite absolute, "Submit, otherwise you will resist God and be judged!" And many stop there. Or they realize that can't be entirely true and look for examples in Scripture where believers have resisted the state to show that Romans 13 needs some qualification.

We will look at some more of these examples in a moment, but first it is important to realize how clearly Paul draws the limits of subjection even here in Romans 13. We don't even have to look anywhere else, it's right here! I admit, it is not immediately obvious. Maybe Paul wrote this a little hidden on purpose so that the Roman state would not understand it should they get their hands on the letter. Whatever the case, we Christians can see it if we take a closer look at the text. So, let's look again at the text and see if we can find these limits.

"Let every person be subject to…any authority?" No, but to the *governing authorities*, that is, only to those who are actually instituted and appointed by God to govern in any particular case. "For there is no authority except from God, and those that exist have been instituted by God. Therefore, whoever resists the authorities resists what God has appointed, and those who resist will incur judgment. For rulers are not a terror to…the one who just always does everything they say, but for the one who resists them?" No, but they are not a terror to *good conduct*, but to *bad*. "Would you have no fear of the one who is in authority? Then… just always do everything they say?" No, but do what is *good*, and you will receive his approval, for he is God's servant for your *good*. "But if you…do not do whatever he asks of you be afraid?" No, but if you do *wrong*, be afraid, for he does not bear the sword in vain. "For he is the servant of God, an avenger who carries out God's wrath on…the one who does not do whatever he demands of him?" No, but on the *wrongdoer*. "Therefore, one must be in subjection…only to avoid God's wrath?" No, not only to avoid

God's wrath but also but also for the sake of conscience. For the conscience distinguishes between *good* and *wrong*.

Do you see what Paul is doing here? Do you see what this is about at its core? It's not about us just doing whatever the state says. It's about us doing what is good and refraining from doing what is wrong! And that, by the way, is exactly what the other passages of Scripture in the New Testament have to say on this subject, *e.g.*, Titus 3:1-2, "Remind them to be submissive to rulers and authorities, to be obedient, to be ready for every *good* work, to speak *evil* of no one." Or 1 Peter 2:13-17:

> Be subject for the Lord's sake to every human institution, whether it be to the emperor as supreme, or to governors as sent by him to punish those who do *evil* and to praise those who do *good*. For this is the will of God, that by doing *good* you should put to silence the ignorance of foolish people. Live as people who are free, not using your freedom as a cover-up for *evil*, but living as servants of God. Honor everyone. Love the brotherhood. Fear God. Honor the emperor.

It's not about just doing everything the state says, it's about doing what's good and not doing what's evil.

And who decides what is good and evil? The state? Everything that the state approves is good, and everything that the state punishes is evil? No, the other way around! That which is good, the state should approve, and that which is evil, the state should punish. Who then decides bindingly for all people and all states what is good and evil? God, of course, and He alone. This is God's prerogative, not the prerogative of a state. That is why Paul goes on to write in Romans 13:8-10:

Owe no one anything, except to love each other, for the one who loves another has fulfilled the law. For the commandments, 'You shall not commit adultery, You shall not murder, You shall not steal, You shall not covet,' and any other commandment, are summed up in this word: 'You shall love your neighbor as yourself.' Love does no wrong to a neighbor; therefore, love is the fulfilling of the law.

Do you see what Paul does immediately? He explains to us what is good and evil: it is the law of God that determines that – not the law of the state. The state is commissioned by God to protect us from adulterers and murderers and thieves and everyone who breaks God's commandments and does not love his neighbor but does evil to him. And whenever the state fulfills its God-given duty, whenever it truly acts as God's servant, it acts in accordance with God's law, praising what is good according to God's standard and punishing what is evil according to God's standard. And then we can submit to the state joyfully, because what the state praises agrees with what God's law requires of us, and what the state punishes agrees with what God's law forbids us to do. You see, this is how God intended it to be. The state is not for our terror but for our good, because it praises us for what God commands us to do and punishes us for what God forbids us to do; and so, it truly acts as God's servant and His avenger.

However, we all know that there are rulers and states that are so ungodly that they no longer fulfill this God-given task but have perverted it. They no longer praise good and punish evil, but they call evil good and good evil; they turn darkness into light and light into darkness; bitter into sweet and sweet into bitter; they praise the wrongdoer and punish the one who does good. We know that, Paul knew that, and most certainly God knows that, for He has judged countless rulers and states for their evil deeds. So, when Paul writes that the state is God's servant and avenger, he is not describing how every state actually *is* at all times, but how the state *should be* according to God's intention. But the state can stray from God's intention and pervert it and turn it into the opposite. When a state acts in this way, it is no longer fulfilling its God-given duty, rather it is acting against God; then it is no longer using the authority God has bestowed upon it, but it is abusing it; then it is no longer a servant of God, but it is a servant of Satan. Of course, even as Satan's servant, the state still remains a servant of God, just as Satan himself is a servant of God – for God still uses them for His purposes – but now no longer for the good of the people, but for their own judgment and destruction.

In fact, no state can completely reject God's mandate. We all live in God's world, and we can violate God's rules only to a certain extent. A state that no longer punishes evil at all cannot long exist, but will quickly perish. That is why, even in the most unjust regimes, murder and theft are still punishable. And that is why, as Christians, we do not resist a state power altogether. We do not say, "Now the state has become so evil that I no longer obey it at all," but we continue to subject ourselves, even to a wicked state, in all things in which it still fulfills its task as God's servant, praising what is good and punishing what is evil, and resist it only in those things where it no longer does so.

You see, there is actually no right of the Christian to resist the state, there is only the duty to resist it. Either the state demands something good from us, something that is in accordance with God's commandments. Then we are obliged to obey the state. Or it demands something evil from us, something that is contrary to God's commandments. Then we are obligated to resist it. So, there is no right to resist, only a duty. Let's be careful not to miss the time when we must resist.

So, when exactly do we need to resist the state? From what has been said so far, we can deduce three categories. We oppose the state: (1) when the state forbids something that God commands; (2) when the state commands something that God forbids; and (3) when the state commands something that it has no God-given authority to command – this last point is a bit more difficult. Let's look at these three points now.

A) WE RESIST WHEN THE STATE FORBIDS SOMETHING THAT GOD COMMANDS

The most famous example of this in the New Testament is probably found in Acts 5, where the apostles are brought before the high council, and the high priest accuses them of teaching in Jesus' name although they had forbidden them to do so. And thereupon it is written in Acts 5:29, "But Peter and the apostles answered, 'We must obey God rather than men.'" God commands us to preach Jesus. When the state forbids us to do so, it is forbidding something that God commands; it is punishing something that is good, and thus it is not acting as God's servant but outside the authority given to it by God, and we must obey God rather than men and resist the state.

Another example is found in Dan. 6:7, where we read that King Darius issues an ordinance and enforces an injunction, "that whoever makes petition to any god or man for thirty days, except to you, O king, shall be cast into the den of lions." How does Daniel respond to this command of the king? We read about this in Daniel 6:10-11,

> When Daniel knew that the document had been signed, he went to his house where he had windows in his upper chamber open toward Jerusalem. He got down on his knees three times a day and prayed and gave thanks before his God, as he had done previously. Then these men came by agreement and found Daniel making petition and plea before his God.

Daniel did not have to think long. God commands him to worship Him; the king forbids it. Daniel obeys God more than men and defies the king; immediately and at the open window so that all can witness it, and is thrown into the lions' den for it. Do you think the state was acting as God's servant, as an avenger, bringing God's wrath upon Daniel for his wrongdoing when it punished him with capital punishment in the lions' den?

Another question: Was Daniel persecuted because of his faith? Many Christians today would have to say: no. After all, they argue in our current situation that we do not have persecution because the state measures are not exclusively directed against believers and are only temporary restrictions. But the king's ordinance was not exclusively directed against Jews either. It affected everyone. And it was limited in time to just thirty days. So, was Daniel not persecuted? Do you see how inconsistent this reasoning is? Of course, Daniel was persecuted. Why? Because he could not obey the king's ordinance *due to his faith* and was therefore punished by the state. This is persecution: when you have to resist the state *because of your faith*, because you know that God's commandments are above those of the state, because you obey God rather than men, and for this you are punished by the state. It doesn't matter if unbelievers are also affected by a measure, because they have no higher authority than the state and can therefore submit, but you cannot and will therefore be punished.

B) WE RESIST WHEN THE STATE COMMANDS SOMETHING THAT GOD FORBIDS

An example of this is found in Daniel 3, where we read how King Nebuchadnezzar has a golden statue made and invites all the dignitaries of his kingdom to its dedication. And then it says in Daniel 3:3-6,

> And the herald proclaimed aloud, 'You are commanded, O peoples, nations, and languages, that when you hear the sound of the horn, pipe, lyre, trigon, harp, bagpipe, and every kind of music, you are to fall down and worship the golden image that King Nebuchadnezzar has set up. And whoever does not fall down and worship shall immediately be cast into a burning fiery furnace.'

And the three friends of Daniel, Shadrach, Meshach, and Abednego, or according to their real names: Hananiah, Mishael, and Azariah, disobey. You have to imagine this scene: Everyone falls down, thousands of people, and three men remain standing! God forbids worshipping other gods or images of gods. When the state commands us to do this, it is commanding something that God forbids, and thus it is not acting as God's servant but outside the authority given to it by God, and we must obey God rather than men and resist the state.

Again, the question: Were Shadrach, Meshach, and Abednego

persecuted because of their faith? After all, the king's command was directed at all people. They all had their own gods and they all had to fall down. But of course, this is persecution because Daniel's three friends could not obey this commandment *because of their faith* and were therefore punished.

Another example are the Hebrew midwives. We read in Exodus 1:15-17,

> Then the king of Egypt said to the Hebrew midwives, one of whom was named Shiphrah and the other Puah, 'When you serve as midwife to the Hebrew women and see them on the birthstool, if it is a son, you shall kill him, but if it is a daughter, she shall live.' But the midwives feared God and did not do as the king of Egypt commanded them, but let the male children live.

Pharaoh commanded something evil, and the midwives resisted. And two verses down, we read that they also lied to Pharaoh, much like Rahab later lied to the state authorities to protect the Israelite scouts. And both the midwives and Rahab are not rebuked for their resistance to the state authority, but commended for their faith and fear of God, and blessed by God.

C) WE RESIST WHEN THE STATE COMMANDS OR FORBIDS SOMETHING THAT IT HAS NO GOD-GIVEN AUTHORITY TO COMMAND OR FORBID

We are subject to the state only to the extent that God has actually given it authority over us. This point is a little more difficult, and I want to divide it into two sub-points:

First, we resist when the state infringes on rights that come to us by nature as creatures made in the image of God. All human beings have inalienable rights by nature, by creation, which no one, not even the state, may infringe upon: the right to work and to provide for oneself and one's family; the right to marry and to celebrate that wedding, not just to sign a piece of paper; the right to have a family and to visit them and hold them in one's arms, as a father to be present at the birth of his child or as a daughter to hold the hand of her dying mother. These things are inherently our rights, which no one may take away from us because we are created in the image of God and these rights are part of the creation mandate. Perhaps today we must also add the right to be able to breathe freely and not to have to wear a piece of cloth in front of our mouth and nose. When the state interferes with these things, which are our natural rights, it is acting satanically, and we must resist.

On the other hand, we resist when the state encroaches on a sphere of authority that God has assigned to someone else. Biblically, a distinction can be made between at least three spheres of authority ordained by God: the family, the church, and the state. The state has no right to interfere in the affairs of any of these other spheres of authority, the family or the church. It must stay out of them completely. However, this does not mean that there can be no overlap of spheres of authority. If the father beats his son to death, then the state must punish him, and the father cannot plead that it is a family matter that is none of the state's business. These are natural overlaps of spheres of authority. But where there is no such overlap, the limits of authority must be respected. In the Bible we have the examples of King Saul and King

Uzziah, both of whom wanted to take over duties that were only the priests'. Both were punished by God for this encroachment into the sphere of authority of the church.

To illustrate this, let me take an example from the spheres of authority of the family and the church. Scripture commands Christians in Hebrews 13:17, "Obey your leaders and submit to them…" So, the members of my church have to obey me and submit to me. This is what the Scripture says. Now, if I were to command the members of my church to eat only chicken soup at home, for breakfast, lunch, and dinner, should they comply and obey me? After all, it is not a sin to eat chicken soup. I may even command it out of loving care, because I am convinced that chicken soup is very healthy. The obvious answer is: No, you must not obey me! Because I would demand something that I am not allowed to demand, because it is outside my sphere of authority, outside the authority that God has given me. If I commanded such a thing, I would be a tyrant and not a servant of God. If a father from my church were to obey me, and there was only chicken soup to eat at his home, he would even sin. Why is that? For three reasons: Firstly, he would be handing over to me the sphere of authority that God has assigned to him for his house, thus acting negligently and unfaithfully. Secondly, he would not love but hate me if he did not admonish me by word and resistance that I must not tyrannically rule over the church members, because, by doing so, I incur God's judgment. And thirdly, he would not love his neighbor either, his brothers and sisters, but would hate them, because he would do nothing to protect them from my tyranny. The same applies to the relationship between the state and the church. Where the state interferes in the church's (or the family's) sphere of authority, we must resist.

But beware: this is not about measures taken by the state that only *indirectly* affect the worship service. The state can require a church to install a new emergency exit in the church building. This is not an encroachment on the sphere of authority of the church but is within the state's authority. It may well mean that five seats are lost as a result. But that is only an indirect consequence that the church must accept. The state does not interfere directly with the sphere of the church; it only does something that may have indirect effects. But what the state may not do is to issue decrees that directly interfere with the church, its faith, its practice or its worship, either in the content of preaching or in the outward form of worship. God has not given the state the authority to do so. Remember, the state is not the highest authority on this earth. I fear that many Christians have unconsciously adopted this secular worldview that there is nothing above the state and therefore the state is allowed to do just about anything. This is not true. High above the state sits God, the only sovereign. And He has merely delegated part of His authority to the state, and only within certain limits.

And if we, as the church, do not resist the encroachments of the state, we sin, just as the father who does not resist my chicken soup diet would sin. Pastors would sin because God has appointed them over the affairs of the church, over the souls of our sheep, and they must give an account to God. If they allow the state to encroach on their God-ordained sphere of authority, they are acting negligently and unfaithfully. And we all sin because we do not love and honor the state as the servant of God. After all, behind the state are people who will eventually face their Creator and have to answer for their actions. We must not simply let them run to their doom, but we must show them, through our resistance, that they must not rule as tyrants, because, by doing so, they will heap up for themselves the wrath of God. Finally, we do not love our neighbor, our brothers and sisters, if we simply allow the state to take away our freedoms without resistance; freedoms for which our brothers and sisters fought and suffered and died in past centuries. Once the state has realized how it can expand its domain without resistance, why shouldn't it continue doing it; why shouldn't it do it again? Our children and grandchildren must then suffer from our failures and cowardice. Therefore, it is unloving toward them if we do not jealously guard our freedoms. As Christians, we obey the state whenever it demands good from us. But we resist the state whenever it demands evil from us and acts as a tyrant. When we do so, we are not resisting God's decree, but affirming it. As the Scottish reformer John Knox said, "Resistance to tyranny is obedience to God."

Christian resistance is always non-violent. We plead, we exhort, we convict, and we refuse to obey. And our resistance is always accompanied by respect, reverence, and prayer for the authorities we have to resist. In Acts 23 we read that the high priest Ananias orders that Paul be struck on the mouth. And then it says in Acts 23:3-5:

> Then Paul said to him, 'God is going to strike you, you whitewashed wall! Are you sitting to judge me according to the law, and yet contrary to the law you order me to be struck?' Those who stood by said, 'Would you revile God's high priest?' And Paul said, 'I did not know, brothers, that he was the high priest, for it is written, 'You shall not speak evil of a ruler of your people.'

The high priest was certainly struck by God, and he was indeed a whitewashed wall. But he was a ruler of the people, and you don't speak of him that way. Dear ones, we must be careful how we speak about our rulers. No matter how vile and ungodly they may be, we must not speak of them disrespectfully, even if we are forced to oppose them.

When we resist the state in this way, it is even a proof of our true submission. If a father wants to do something evil, if he wants to set his house on fire with his wife and daughters inside, shouldn't his sons stand in his way and stop him? Wouldn't that be the very proof of their loving submission? And would it not be unloving and rebellious to let the father have his way? It is true submission when we resist the state in this way.

A special duty to resist is incumbent on those who themselves hold a subordinate state office, the so-called "lesser magistrates." If our governor realizes that the decisions of the federal government are evil, he must not implement them in his state. If a policeman realizes that his orders are evil, he must not enforce them. He must say, "No, I'm not breaking up this worship service, I'm not imposing this fine, I'm not taking this pastor to the police station." It is their duty to resist and protect those who are subordinate to them.

Even when we have to resist, we do so in an attitude of submission. And that also means that we willingly bear the consequences of our resistance. For we must be aware: The state carries the sword, and it can use it, and it can misuse it. It can fire the policeman who resists, it can fine us and ruin us economically, it can throw us in jail, like our brother Pastor James Coates, and it can even kill us. We need not be afraid of this, because then the state does not act as God's servant, not as God's avenger. That is not the wrath of God that comes upon us. That is the state acting against God and misusing the sword. Even if the state abuses its authority and comes against us, we know that our Lord is given all authority in heaven and on earth. He can override the judgment of the state. He saved Daniel from the lions' den and his three friends from the fiery furnace when the state wanted to kill them. He protected and blessed the Hebrew midwives and Rahab. But often the Lord decrees that we must suffer if we rightfully resist the state.

The apostle James was killed with the sword by King Herod, we know that from the Scriptures. And according to church tradition, the other apostles did not fare any better: Peter was crucified upside-down on an X-shaped cross in Rome. Matthew was killed with a sword in Ethiopia. John was boiled in a bath of boiling oil in Rome at the time of the persecution. He miraculously survived and was exiled to the island of Patmos. James, the Lord's brother, was thrown from the southeast pinnacle of the temple when he refused to renounce his faith in Christ. When it was discovered that he had survived the fall, his enemies beat him to death with a club. Bartholomew was a missionary to Asia. He witnessed to the Word of God in what is now Turkey and was tortured, scourged, and skinned for his preaching in Armenia. Andrew was crucified on an X-shaped cross in Greece after being cruelly flogged by soldiers. Hanging on the cross, he preached to his tormentors for two more days until he died. Thomas was stabbed with a spear during one of his missionary journeys to India, where he wanted to plant churches. Matthias, the apostle chosen to replace Judas Iscariot, was stoned and beheaded. The apostle Paul was imprisoned several times, tortured, and beheaded by Emperor Nero in Rome in A.D. 67. We cannot say for sure if every detail of this is true, but it is clear in which tradition we stand. And countless other martyrs could be listed. Many of them resisted the state and were imprisoned, tortured, and killed for it. They took up their cross and followed Jesus. But not one of them ever regretted their decision. For they obeyed God and entrusted themselves to Him who judges justly.

Let us not cease to work the good, and joyfully be willing to suffer persecution for it, when necessary. Thus did the apostles. We read about this in Acts 5:40-42:

> and when they had called in the apostles, they beat them and charged them not to speak in the name of Jesus, and let them go. Then they left the presence of the council, rejoicing that they were counted worthy to suffer dishonor for the name. And every day, in the temple and from house to house, they did not cease teaching and preaching that the Christ is Jesus."

The state forbids you to do something good, you resist the state and continue to do the good, the state punishes you, you rejoice and continue to do what the state has forbidden you. This is Christian resistance.

Let us be encouraged by the words of our Lord, in Revelation 2:10, "Do not fear what you are about to suffer. Behold, the devil is about to throw some of you into prison, that you may be tested, and for ten days you will have tribulation. Be faithful unto death, and I will give you the crown of life." Amen.

– Part 3 –

Guidance for a Biblical Approach to the Covid Vaccines

Tobias Riemenschneider and Peter Schild

Preface

Each one should be fully convinced in his own mind. (…) For whatever does not proceed from faith is sin. (Romans 14:5b.23b)

This guidance is intended for Christians who refuse Corona vaccination for reasons of faith or conscience, or who are struggling with the question of whether or not to be vaccinated, but also contains important information for Christians who have already been vaccinated. We know of many brothers and sisters in German-speaking countries who refuse vaccination and are therefore confronted with existential worries and increasingly have to struggle with fear and despondency. They are often abandoned by their own churches and pastors, who cannot understand their plight or even exclude them from the worship service and the fellowship of the saints. For many Christians, this is the most difficult test of faith they have ever experienced.

This guidance was born out of a deeply felt desire not to leave these brothers and sisters alone in their distress, but to stand by them with biblical counsel and encouragement, and comfort them during this difficult time.

1. Current Situation

The pressure on people who do not want to be vaccinated against Corona or who have concerns about the vaccines has reached an unbearable level. Unvaccinated people are largely excluded from social and economic life, and now also from working life, or have to buy their way in by taking daily tests; depending on the federal state, this also applies to worship services. Recently, German Health Minister Jens Spahn announced that 2G ("*Geimpft oder Genesen,*" in English: vaccinated or recovered; *i.e.*, admission only for people who have been vaccinated or recently recovered from a covid infection) would possibly apply everywhere except city halls and supermarkets for the entire year 2022 and beyond, regardless of how low the incidence of Corona infections would be. At the same time, the ubiquitous state and media propaganda portrays the unvaccinated as scapegoats who, because of their alleged unreasonableness and recklessness, are to blame for the rising numbers of infections and the sometimes tyrannical measures taken by the state, which is presented as having no alternative, thus fomenting hatred of the unvaccinated and dividing our society.

Since the constantly increased pressure to be vaccinated is not sufficient to make everyone compliant, vaccine mandates have now been announced for certain sectors, which is likely to result in a number of people, unwilling to submit to the tyranny, losing their jobs. The imminent introduction of vaccine mandates for the entire population, as recently decided in Austria, possibly including children, can now also be regarded as almost certain. Even Chancellor-designate Olaf Scholz, who only a few weeks ago had spoken out against vaccine mandates, now wants to initiate a legislative process to introduce vaccine mandates.

It can be assumed that more and more people will no longer be able to withstand the pressure and will be coerced into getting vaccinated. How can Christians, who have so far rejected vaccination for reasons of faith or conscience, now behave?

2. Principle: Vaccinations as a Decision of Conscience

Since the Holy Scriptures do not contain any commandments that universally stipulate whether a Christian may be vaccinated or not, this decision is, in principle, left to the conscience of each Christian. Therefore, Christians can come to different conclusions. However, this does not mean that one can decide as one pleases. Rather, each Christian must carefully examine the criteria known to him or her that are essential for the decision and weigh them against each other, applying biblical commandments and principles. If one is then fully convinced in one's own mind, one can act by faith.[1] So what are the criteria we as Christians need to consider when deciding whether to get vaccinated?

3. Criteria for a Biblical Decision of Conscience

A) Vaccination as the way out

Very soon after the beginning of the Corona crisis, vaccination

---

1 *Cf.* Rom. 14:5b.23b.

was declared as the only way out of the crisis. If the Corona cult was a new religion, vaccination would be its way of salvation. Now, Christians may be tempted to seek their way out in vaccination as well, given the unbearable pressure, the robbery of their freedoms, the permanent branding and discrimination by the state, the media, society, employers, work colleagues, family, and possibly their own church, as well as the fear of losing their livelihood and of coercive measures by the state. Perhaps the thought is growing louder and louder, "Just a little jab for my freedom!"

We must be aware that it will not be done with one injection. Current infection figures show that people who have received two injections are by no means persistently immune. Meanwhile, even politicians admit that the injections neither provide lasting self-protection against Corona infection nor reliably prevent infection of other people, but only reduce the risk of a severe course of the disease for the vaccinated person. In addition, mutations of the virus, which may be facilitated precisely by mass vaccination, are likely to further reduce the effectiveness of vaccinations.

Instead of thinking about alternatives to vaccination, however, salvation is sought in more vaccinations. So now the third injection is propagated; in Israel already the fourth. It is unlikely that permanent immunity will be achieved after these injections. Rather, we must assume that new injections will be demanded regularly, probably every six months, in order to buy one's freedoms and respect by society, and this for years. Federal Health Minister Jens Spahn has already announced that only those who have been "booster vaccinated" will be considered vaccinated. The president of the World Medical Association, Frank Ulrich Montgomery, also recently stated that it will be necessary to "vaccinate the world for years to come." So, you don't just opt for one jab, but possibly a long-lasting system of constantly recurring injections.

Since vaccinated individuals are still part of the infectious process, future restrictions, such as lockdowns, cannot be ruled out even if the population is fully vaccinated, as currently shown by the example of Gibraltar, where the population is fully vaccinated and yet events for Christmas are being cancelled or restricted due to the highest incidence figures since the beginning of the crisis.

B) USE OF EMBRYONIC CELL LINES

As far as is known, all Corona vaccines currently in use in Germany have been developed, manufactured, or tested using embryonic cell lines. These cell lines were grown from tissue of aborted children whose organs were "harvested" for this purpose under cruel conditions. How many children were killed for these experiments is not known. In one case, the inventor of the rubella vaccine, Dr. Stanley Plotkin, admitted to "using up" more than seventy children for his research on vaccine development.

God commands us not to murder (Ex. 20:13; Deuteronomy 5:17). This also applies to children in the womb (Ex. 21:22-25), whose inward parts the LORD forms and who He knits in His image (Ps. 139:13; Genesis 1:27). Moreover, we have the commandment not to participate in the sins of others either, such as the abortionist doctors or the vaccine developers (1 Tim. 5:22; Rev. 18:4). Embryonic cell lines are also used in other medicines and vaccines that we have already taken, possibly unknowingly. This does not absolve us, however, now that we know about the use of such cell lines, from examining whether we can reconcile it with our conscience and before God to take such vaccines. We must ask ourselves whether we are ultimately profiting indirectly from the murder of numerous children and the theft of their organs.

C) HEALTH RISKS OF THE VACCINES

The commandment "You shall not murder" includes, in principle, other harm to the body or health. God made the bodies of human beings, and the bodies of Christians are especially the temple of God (1 Cor. 3:16.17), and we have no right to harm them. This also applies to our own body (Eph. 5:29).

While politicians and the media warn massively about the dangers of a Corona infection, hardly any information is provided about the possible dangers of the vaccines. However, in order to be able to make a well-founded decision, these should also be seriously considered.

The vaccines are a novel, gene-based technology that has never been approved for use in humans and whose test phases have been extremely shortened (telescoped) compared to those of all other vaccines that have been approved to date. Therefore, no reliable statements can yet be made about their possible side effects and long-term consequences. Various side effects, some of them severe and relatively frequent, are already known, such as thrombosis or inflammation of the heart muscle (myocarditis). Due to insufficient data, a high number of unreported cases can be assumed. In addition, some scientists warn that the vaccinations, especially if they are repeated continuously, can lead to antibody-dependent enhancement (ADE), which can lead to more severe courses of disease in the case of a Corona infection, so that the intended protective effect of the vaccinations could be reversed.

Each Christian must therefore weigh up, to the best of his or her knowledge, whether for him or her personally the risk of a possible COVID-19 infection outweighs the risk of the vaccines. Such a weighing may be against the vaccination in many cases due to the lack of safety data on side effects and long-term consequences of the vaccinations; this is especially true for younger, healthy individuals, for whom a COVID-19 infection is relatively harmless (the median age of those who died "of or with" Covid in Germany is about 83 years, which is above the average life expectancy), and for convalescents who have natural immunity to COVID-19. For the elderly, the risk assessment may be different.

Moreover, we bear responsibility not only for ourselves, but also for our children. For children, an infection with COVID-19 is almost completely harmless. Vaccination of children can therefore not be justified against the background of the possible side effects of the injections. The objection that children could infect their grandparents, for whom a COVID-19 infection could then be more dangerous, is not valid because the injections do not effectively prevent transmission of the virus. In any case, the health of elders should not be bought at the cost of the health of children and grandchildren. This is morally reprehensible.

D) SUBMISSION TO LIES AND TYRANNY

The Corona crisis is characterized on the part of the state by deception, propaganda, blatant lies, fear-mongering, and drastic censorship, as well as the deprivation of God-given and constitutionally enshrined freedoms, as a result of which, countless people are severely harmed in a variety of ways economically, socially, health-wise, and mentally. The fact that this is done under the pretext of protecting life should not surprise us, because our Lord

Himself teaches us that the kings of the Gentiles exercise lordship over them, and those in authority over them are called benefactors (Luke 22:25).

Regarding the vaccines, for example, we were told that it would be possible to return to normality when a vaccine was available; then that this would only be possible when all those willing to be vaccinated had been offered vaccination; then that this would only be possible when herd immunity had been achieved as a result of a vaccination rate of about two-thirds of the population. Now vaccine mandates for the entire population are announced, which, according to earlier statements by top politicians, would never happen.[2]

There would not be enough space to list all the lies in this Corona crisis. Why, for example, were hospitals in Germany shut down and thousands of intensive care units cut in the midst of this "epidemic of national magnitude"? Are the unvaccinated really to blame when the health care system reaches its limits, or not rather the health care crisis caused by cutbacks, hospital closures, staff shortages, and poor working conditions, which have been criticized for decades? Or how can it be justified that unvaccinated individuals, who have proven by a negative test that they are not infectious, are excluded from events, while vaccinated individuals who have not been tested and are possibly infectious, are admitted? This has nothing to do with science or reason, but with

---

2 For example, on May 5, 2020, the Governor of Saxony, Michael Kretschmer, described rumors about vaccine mandates as nonsense. No one would be vaccinated against their will in the Federal Republic of Germany. Also, the rumor that those who do not get vaccinated should lose their constitutional rights would just be immense nonsense and an absurd and malicious assertion; such people should be confronted collectively, he said. Especially in view of Germany's past, compulsory vaccination would be unimaginable.

the enforcement of a political agenda, namely the vaccination of the entire population.

At the same time, censorship has reached a level usually seen only in dictatorships. Even videos by renowned experts who have been considered luminaries in their field for decades are immediately deleted as "fake news" if they contradict the official Corona narrative. This alone should make one suspicious, because the truth would not need to shy away from open discourse.

As Christians, we are to love the truth and walk in the truth,[3] for our Lord is the Truth (John 14:6), and His Word is truth (John 17:17). We must therefore not believe lies and live by lies; rather we are obliged to examine and evaluate the statements of godless politicians and scientists who even deny the Creator Himself. Of course, this also applies *vice versa* to statements made by people who are critical of government actions. Thus, Christians should be especially wary of following preachers who speak against the measures but advocate heresies in other areas.

In addition to lies, the state subdues people with systematic and often arbitrary spreading of fear and terror through ever-new announcements of deadly mutations, forecasts of extreme death rates, and the imminent collapse of the health care system. The state then uses this terror to deprive people of their God-given and constitutionally enshrined rights and liberties through constantly changing, draconian measures for almost two years now.

Now, with vaccination, the state does not even stop at people's bodies, but coerces them into getting injections against their will. At this point, the state interferes with the constitutionally protect-

---

[3] Phil. 4:8; 2 John 1:4; 3 John 1:3; in John's epistles, while the primary concern is to walk in the truth of the gospel, this also precludes living in other lies.

ed right to bodily integrity, thereby overstepping its God-given authority, because our bodies do not belong to the state, but to the Lord who made them and chose them as His temple (1 Cor. 3:16.17; 6:19). However, we must not give to Caesar what is God's (Matt. 22:21; Luke 20:25).

This is an attack on man as being made in the image of God by granting him his freedoms and his dignity as a human being only to the extent that, and for as long as, he fulfills the conditions imposed by the state. Anyone who refuses to comply is degraded to a second-class human being, ostracized by society and granted only what is necessary for survival. This dehumanization is reminiscent of dictatorships of the past, as some people who have experienced the Nazi regime or the communist regimes of the USSR or the GDR confirm. The protection of people through constitutional rights was supposed to prevent such a thing from ever happening again.

Even if one is of the opinion that the measures, such as vaccination, are actually sensible and useful, it cannot be justified biblically that the state has the authority to mandate such measures by force and thus to interfere with the God-given dignity of human beings, which finds its expression, for example, in the right to freedom, to work, to respect, to one's own body, and in the freedom of faith and conscience.

If we decide to get vaccinated, then we must examine whether we can reconcile it with our conscience to submit to this anti-Christian system of lies and tyranny and thereby possibly acknowledge its legitimacy, or whether it is not rather resistance to tyranny that is obedience to God. Moreover, it is to be feared that the state will demand more and more from people if they want to keep their freedoms, as has happened again and again in the last twenty-one months. We must therefore ask ourselves where we see the red line that we will not cross. There is a danger that we will always give in a little bit more and push that red line further and further back.

E) THE MARK OF THE BEAST?

In light of the above, the question arises for many whether the vaccination could be the mark of the beast (Rev. 14:9-13). We do not believe that the mark of the beast necessarily requires a visible mark on the forehead or hand. Rather, Revelation draws from the Old Testament. The Israelites were to bind the commandments of the LORD as a sign on their hand, and it was to be between their eyes as frontlets Deut. 6:4-9). So, they should think and act as God commands in His Word. On the other hand, those who think and act like the beast take on its mark. The image of the beast also draws from the Old Testament, which depicts states hostile to God as beasts (Dan. 7). Therefore, whoever does not think and act according to the truth and the holy commandments of God, but according to the lies and the godless commandments of the antichristian state, takes the mark of the beast (Rev. 13:17). Here, too, parallels to the current situation are undeniable.

Moreover, parallels in church history are striking. The Roman emperor Decius (†251) issued a general decree of sacrifice in early 250 that required every citizen of the Roman Empire to appear before a commission to sacrifice to the emperor. For this they received a written confirmation, the *libellus*. Anyone who refused to sacrifice to the emperor and could not produce a *libellus* was considered an enemy of the state and faced arrest, forced labor, deprivation of property, banishment, or death. Since Christians could not submit to the sacrifice decree, there was a bloody persecution of Christians. Christians who bowed to the pressure and offered the sacrifice were considered apostates (*lapsi*). What was disputed was how to deal with those who had obtained the *libellus* without sacrificing (*libellatici*), since they too gave the impression to others that they had sacrificed to the gods.

Even if we do not believe that the vaccination itself is the mark of the beast or that a Christian who is vaccinated is necessarily apostate, we must ask ourselves what governs our thoughts and actions when we decide to be vaccinated, and whether we thereby obey the state in a sinful way because we acknowledge it as lord over our freedom, our bodies, and ultimately our likeness to God, thus giving to it what is God's alone. Shouldn't we at least consider the vaccination (and certain other government measures) as a test run? If we cannot withstand the pressure and fear of loss now, will we be able to withstand it when it will get even worse?

F) THE COMMANDMENT OF LOVE OF NEIGHBOR

The commandment to love one's neighbor is often cited as an argument in favor of the vaccination. In order to protect their neighbor from infection and prevent hospitals from being overburdened, Christians are required to get vaccinated, they say. We consider this a twisting of the truth. The very premise is a twofold lie. For one thing, the vaccination does not effectively prevent the infection of others, but at best reduces one's own risk of severe courses of the disease. For another, the commandment to love one's neighbor does not mean that every individual must do everything possible to abstractly and potentially reduce the risk of a collective, possibly even at the expense of their own health or the integrity of his conscience.

Moreover, it seems evident to us that most people do not take the vaccine at all to protect others, but to protect themselves. The argument of love of neighbor is therefore hypocritical and moralizing in this context, and no Christian should let this weigh down their conscience. We live up to the commandment to love our neighbor, as we have for millennia, by taking care not to infect others when we are actually ill or likely to be infectious.

If one wants to cite the commandment of love of neighbor, then one can even turn it around and argue to the effect that resistance to freedom-robbing and tyrannical measures of the state is precisely an expression of love of neighbor, since I do not want to tolerate the violation of my neighbor's rights of freedom and his dignity and want to protect him from existential hardship, hatred, and discrimination. Resistance to tyranny is thus also a fight for my neighbor as well as for our children and our children's children, so that they too can live in a free country where their rights, their faith, and their conscience are protected.

However, in special cases, love of neighbor can indeed speak in favor of vaccination, namely, if vaccination itself is not seen as an act of love of neighbor, but as a means to an end in order to be able to do works of love of neighbor, because that is love of neighbor rightly understood. For example, someone who can only visit his sick mother in hospital with proof of vaccination, or who does not want to lose his job so that he can continue to provide for his family, his pastors, or other brothers and sisters (see below), or who wants to keep his job in an old people's home because he wants to continue to care for people and bring them the hope of the gospel, or who wants to travel to a foreign country to preach the gospel there as a missionary, may have good reasons that justify his getting vaccinated. However, the argument of love for neighbor must not be misused as a pious pretext.

G) IMPACT ON BROTHERS AND SISTERS AND THE CHURCH

Finally, in making our decision, we must consider the possible effects on our brothers and sisters and our church. Vaccination carries the great risk of leading to division even in those churches that have so far been able to maintain unity, for the following reasons:

Those who refuse to be vaccinated because of their convictions of faith and conscience, and who have existential worries because of this, or who actually experience existential hardships because they lose their jobs, for example, or face compulsory fines or imprisonment and, in the end, possibly compulsory vaccination, may feel abandoned and betrayed in their greatest of hardships by brothers and sisters who have opted for vaccination as an "easy way out," or may despise them as unspiritual, cowardly, unfaithful, or even apostate.

On the other hand, those who are vaccinated may no longer understand the existential worries of their brothers and sisters and may no longer sympathize with them, because these worries are no longer part of their own reality. In addition, vaccinated believers might be pressured by their own consciences to justify themselves when they see their brethren suffering for their beliefs while they themselves have evaded suffering. The vaccinated might then despise the unvaccinated brothers and sisters as proud because they suffer unnecessarily in order to stand out as more holy.

The only way out we see for churches is a mutual commitment of brothers and sisters not to despise each other because of their decision to be or not to be vaccinated, and a commitment of brothers and sisters who are vaccinated to comfort those who face hardships because of their decision not to be vaccinated, because they lose their jobs, for example, and to contribute to their care. Just as Obadiah did, using his privileged position in the king's court to hide a hundred prophets of the Lord and provide them with bread and water (1 Kgs. 18:4). For if a brother or sister is poorly clothed and lacking in daily food, and one of you says to them, "Go in peace, be warmed and filled," without giving them the things needed for the body, what good is that (James 2:15-16)? And if anyone has the world's goods and sees his brother in need, yet closes his heart against him, how does God's love abide in him (1 John 3:17)? For we ought to lay down our lives for the brothers (1 John 3:16). May what is written of the first Christians also apply to us, "Now the full number of those who believed were of one heart and soul, and no one said that any of the things that belonged to him was his own, but they had everything in common" (Acts 4:32).

As pastors, we will be careful to uphold these commitments in order to prevent division in the church.

4. Excursus: 3G/2G in Churches[4]

Churches that strictly follow 3G or 2G regulations and exclude brothers and sisters from participation in worship and brotherly fellowship because of a lack of test or vaccination proof are sinning. Whether someone is allowed to worship God in the

---

4   3G: Access only for vaccinated, recently recovered, or tested persons ("*geimpft, genesen oder getestet*"); 2G: Access only for vaccinated or recently recovered persons ("*geimpft oder genesen*").

congregation must not be made dependent on their vaccination status or a health certificate. Pastors have no right to domineer over Christ's blood-bought flock and bind the consciences of the brethren by making man's commandments a prerequisite for participation in the congregations and worship of God.

Christ, not Caesar, is the Head of the church. He alone determines under what conditions someone may come to Him; and He calls to Himself through His holy gospel all who labor and are heavy laden (Matt. 11:28), not only those who have been vaccinated or tested or have recovered, and promises not to cast out anyone who comes to Him (John 6:37). Those who let the state determine under what conditions someone has access to worship are giving to Caesar what is God's. No shepherd has the right to cast out a sheep when the Chief Shepherd has promised to accept it.

Every pastor must be aware that he will have to give an account – not to the state, but to God – of how he has kept watch over the souls of the sheep entrusted to his care (Heb. 13:17). Should we pastors not be ready to be condemned by earthly judges, if in return we will one day receive our reward as good and faithful servants before the judgment seat of Christ? But what will be the judgment on those who have followed the counsel of the world and erected a "dividing wall" in His holy church instead of preserving the unity of the Spirit (Eph. 4:3)?

Brothers and sisters who are part of such a church should seriously consider whether they can participate in this injustice or should not join a faithful church to be able to survive these dark times.

5. Concrete Courses of Action

The decision to be vaccinated, or not, is a decision of conscience that each Christian must make for himself or herself after serious and careful consideration of the above criteria in accordance with Scripture and after consultation with his or her pastors. A Christian must not allow himself to be coerced by pressure and threats into doing something against his conscience. As Martin Luther also said, at the Diet of Worms, when it was a matter of life and death for him, "Since my conscience is captive to the word of God, I cannot and will not recant anything because it is dangerous and impossible to do anything against one's conscience. God help me. Amen." Anyone who, after careful consideration, comes to the conclusion that he wishes to be vaccinated, and can do so in faith and without doubt, should not be despised by any other Christian for doing so.

Even if a Christian allows himself to be unjustifiably vaccinated, even if it is only out of weakness, because he can no longer withstand the pressure, he may have sinned because he did not do it with a clear conscience and out of faith; as the body of Christ we want to welcome the weak in faith, but not to quarrel over opinions (Rom. 14:1). On the other hand, the one who has been vaccinated must not despise the other brothers and sisters, but is obliged to use the advantages he has gained through vaccination for the good of the brothers and sisters, so that there is no division in the body.

For those Christians who conclude that they do not want to give in to the pressure and remain unvaccinated, we currently see the following three possible outcomes:

A) SUFFERING

For one thing, we can suffer the consequences of our resistance, which does not mean that we cannot fight back with the means at our disposal to prevent harm to ourselves or our family, such as by exploring the possibility of obtaining a medical certificate confirming that you cannot receive the vaccination for health reasons, taking legal action, or participating in political actions such as rallies or a general strike.

When we refuse the vaccination for reasons of faith and conscience, we suffer for Christ's sake, and therefore we can do so without fear, casting all our anxieties upon the Lord, for He cares for us (1 Peter 5:7). We may be hated and reviled, incited against and segregated, and shut up in our houses. But Jesus tells us, "Blessed are you when people hate you and when they exclude you and revile you and spurn your name as evil, on account of the Son of Man!" (Luke 6:22).

We may also not be able to complete our studies, or lose our job and thereby our livelihood, and perhaps our house, and may not even be allowed to enter a grocery store at some point. But Jesus speaks, "do not seek what you are to eat and what you are to drink, nor be worried. For all the nations of the world seek after these things, and your Father knows that you need them. Instead, seek his kingdom, and these things will be added to you. Fear not, little flock, for it is your Father's good pleasure to give you the kingdom'" (Luke 12:29-32; also see Ps. 37:25).

In all of this, we can wait for the help of our God with prayer and fasting, for our help comes from the Lord who made heaven and earth (Ps. 121:2). Perhaps He will provide a way out. For example, a conventional inactivated vaccine against Corona could be approved that neither has a genetic mode of action nor uses embryonic cell lines[5] and therefore eliminates at least some of the concerns listed above.

But it may also be that the Lord has determined not to create such a way out, but has decreed that things will get worse and the state will introduce a general vaccine mandate. Then it may be that the state will impose fines on us that will ruin us financially; but we will joyfully accept the plundering of our property, since we know that we ourselves have a better possession and an abiding one (Heb. 10:34b). Then it may also be that the state casts us into prison, as the Austrian government's bill already provides for.[6] But Jesus speaks, "Do not fear what you are about to suffer. Behold, the devil is about to throw some of you into prison, that you may be tested, and for ten days you will have tribulation. Be faithful unto death, and I will give you the crown of life" (Rev. 2:10).

Finally, it may also be that the state will forcibly vaccinate us. If this should come so, then we may submit without fear and with confidence in the Lord, since it is then no longer our decision. We would when reviled, not revile in return; suffering, not threaten, but continue entrusting ourselves to Him who judges justly (1 Peter 2:23).

Since the vaccination in itself does not constitute a denial of the Lord, if the state imposes coercive measures against him, every Christian must examine himself before God as to whether and at what point he wishes to submit to them, in order, for example, to be able to continue to provide his family with the necessities of

---

5   Whether this will then actually be the case with an inactivated vaccine remains to be seen.

6   § 7 para. 1,2 of the Austrian draft COVID-19 Vaccination Act.

life.

Even if the Lord does not send us salvation here on earth, we need not be afraid of the tyrants, but can be courageous and strong like Shadrach, Meshach, and Abednego, who even under the greatest pressure did not allow themselves to be forced to sin, but said to the king, who was filled with rage and threatened them with a cruel death:

> We have no need to answer you in this matter. If this be so, our God whom we serve is able to deliver us from the burning fiery furnace, and he will deliver us out of your hand, O king. But if not, be it known to you, O king, that we will not serve your gods or worship the golden image that you have set up" (Dan. 3:16-18).

B) DECEPTION[7]

The Scriptures give us examples in which godly people, in the greatest need to protect their own lives or the lives of others, used deception against their oppressors (1 Sam. 16:1 *et seqq.*; (1 Sam. 21:14). So Rahab lied to the men of the king of Jericho to protect the Israelite spies (Josh. 2:3 *et seqq.*), and so the Hebrew midwives Shiphrah and Puah lied to Pharaoh about why they did not kill the sons of the Hebrew women (Ex. 1:15 *et seqq.*). A well-known example from history is the Christian Corrie ten Boom, who hid Jews during the Nazi rule in the Netherlands, and deceived the tyrannical state in order to save their lives. Many more such examples could be cited. Scripture does not explicitly call us to pretend

---

[7] For the avoidance of doubt, no case has actually been brought to our attention where we have advised a ruse.

or deceive others in such situations, but neither does it rebuke the men and women who did such things in faith and out of fear of God, but presents them to us as heroes of faith (Ex. 1:20.21; Josh. 6:25; Heb. 11:31; James 2:25).

As Christians, we should always prefer the path of truthfulness, even in emergency situations. However, it may be that a Christian is compelled to use cunning for his protection or for the protection of his family or for the fulfillment of other high-ranking commandments of God. We warn, however, that this should not be done lightly, for example in order to be able to participate in social life again, but whoever decides to do this must be completely convinced in his own mind and act by faith, so that he does not sin. Insofar as a Christian has chosen this path, he is obliged to provide for his brothers and sisters who suffer hardships as a result of their resistance, as shown above.

C) FLIGHT

We also consider it a biblical course to flee from tyranny by emigrating to another country. Fleeing need not be a sin; rather, Scripture has several examples of godly and courageous men who fled.[8] In some cases, flight is even commanded by the Lord (Matt.; 24:16; Mark 13:14; Luke 21:21). Especially, those who have children may think about fleeing. This is all the more true if vaccine mandates for children should be introduced.

However, there are some important things to consider here. For one thing, you can only flee if you do not leave anyone unprovided for, for whom you are responsible. For example, if you

---

8   Cf. Genesis 27:43 et seqq.; 1 Sam. 19:10 et seqq.; 2 Sam. 15:14; Jer. 26:21; 1 Kgs. 19:3; Matt. 10:23; Acts 9:25; 12:17; 2 Cor. 11:33.

have an elderly mother or are caring for a sick person, you cannot flee without them unless you have made sure that they will be taken care of. The same applies to pastors, who are responsible for the care of their church and must not abandon their flock when it is in danger (John 10:11-13). In addition, the effects of a flight on the brothers and sisters and the church, who could be disheartened by this, should also be considered. Therefore, flight should not be made without prior consultation with the pastors and the church.

If you decide to flee, you should make sure to look for a place where there is a Bible-believing church that holds services in a language you understand, or at least can offer an appropriate translation, and where there are brothers and sisters who can support you, for example, in finding a job or dealing with the authorities. It is therefore a good idea to discuss the flight in advance with the pastors of this church.

Finally, you have to keep in mind that you cannot know whether you will be permanently safe in the country you are fleeing to. It is possible that vaccine mandates will be introduced there too sooner or later. For instance, EU Commission President Ursula von der Leyen has announced that she wants to consider vaccine mandates for the entire European Union. Therefore, even if we flee, we must not put our hope in a new land, but in the Lord alone, for here we have no lasting city (Heb. 13:14).

6. A Word of Comfort

Beloved brethren, we must be prepared to face difficult times in which Christians, who cannot submit to certain orders of the state for reasons of faith and conscience, will suffer persecution.

The Lord is leading His church into a fiery ordeal in which our faith will be purified so that it will prove true. It is also possible that our church services will no longer be possible in the same form as before. Ultimately, however, we will only return to the state of affairs that was normal for many Christians in many places, at all times. As Paul says, "Indeed, all who desire to live a godly life in Christ Jesus will be persecuted" (2 Tim. 3:12).

Whatever may come and whatever we may have to suffer: We need not fear, for to our Lord has been given all authority in heaven and on earth (Matt. 28:18), and even the state can only do what the Lord permits it to do (John 19:11). If the Lord is our light and our salvation, whom shall we fear? If He is the stronghold of our life, of whom shall we be afraid (Ps. 27:1)? If He is on our side, what can man do to us (Ps. 118:6)? Why should we fear those who kill the body, and after that have nothing more that they can do (Luke 12:4)? Though the nations and the kings of the earth rage, He who sits in the heavens laughs; the Lord holds them in derision (Ps. 2:1 *et seqq.*). In fact, we are witnessing God's wrath right now against the ungodliness and unrighteousness of the nations that He has given up (Rom. 1:28), so we can give glory to the Lord as the righteous judge of the earth.

Even though God's wrath is not for His children, it may well be a chastening for us. Perhaps we have grown too fond of the world. Perhaps we have sought too much distraction in the pleasures of the world. Perhaps we have striven too hard for success and career. Perhaps we have put too much faith in our jobs. For us Christians, this is an opportunity to die more to the world and its desires and to await the coming of our Lord Jesus more joyfully. Let us encourage one another with these words, that the Lord Himself will descend from heaven with a cry of command, with the voice of an archangel, and with the sound of the trumpet of God, and so we will always be with Him (1 Thes. 4:16-18).

In these dark times, let us diligently repent and humble ourselves before the Lord with fervent prayer and fasting, pleading that He may provide salvation for us with a strong hand and an outstretched arm! Let us be filled with the Spirit, addressing one another in psalms and hymns and spiritual songs, singing and making melody to the Lord with your heart! And let us be diligent to love one another, to hold fast to one another, and to live holy lives in obedience to God's commandments, as it is written,

> Let brotherly love continue. Do not neglect to show hospitality to strangers, for thereby some have entertained angels unawares. Remember those who are in prison, as though in prison with them, and those who are mistreated, since you also are in the body. Let marriage be held in honor among all, and let the marriage bed be undefiled, for God will judge the sexually immoral and adulterous. Keep your life free from love of money, and be content with what you have, for he has said, 'I will never leave you nor forsake you.' So we can confidently say, 'The Lord is my helper; I will not fear; what can man do to me?' (Heb. 13:1-6)

Whatever happens, let us never forget to praise our Lord! The prophet Habakkuk experienced a time when God's blessings had departed from the land and people were facing existential hardships because there was no more food. He writes, "Though the fig tree should not blossom, nor fruit be on the vines, the produce of the olive fail and the fields yield no food, the flock be cut off from the fold and there be no herd in the stalls, yet I will rejoice in the

Lord; I will take joy in the God of my salvation. God, the Lord, is my strength" (Hab. 3:17-19a). Let us also rejoice in the Lord and take joy in the God of our salvation, for the Lord is

– Part 4 –

Mandatory Vaccination and the Christian Conscience – an Urgent Plea

Tobias Riemenschneider

Dear Mr. President Dr. Steinmeier,
Dear Mrs. President of the German Parliament Bas,
Dear Mr. Chancellor Scholz,
Dear Mr. Federal Minister of Health Prof. Lauterbach,
Dear Mr. Federal Minister of Justice Dr. Buschmann,
Dear Sirs and Madams Ministers of the Federal Government,
Dear Mr. Governor Kretschmann,
Dear Mr. Governor Dr. Söder,
Dear Mrs. Governing Mayor Dr. Giffey,
Dear Mr. Governor Dr. Woidke,
Dear Mr. President of the Senate and Mayor Dr. Bovenschulte,
Dear Mr. First Mayor Dr. Tschentscher,
Dear Mr. Governor Bouffier,
Dear Mrs. Governor Schwesig,
Dear Mr. Governor Weil,
Dear Mr. Governor Wüst,
Dear Mrs. Governor Dreyer,

Dear Mr. Governor Hans,
Dear Mr. Governor Kretschmer,
Dear Mr. Governor Dr. Haseloff,
Dear Mr. Governor Günther,
Dear Mr. Governor Ramelow,
Dear Sirs and Madams Members of the German Parliament,

WE ARE WRITING TO YOU as pastors, preachers, as well as leaders and staff of Christian churches and ministries and other concerned people who together represent numerous Christians from all over Germany.

As Christians, we are convinced that we must be subject to the governmental authority, since the Bible teaches that all governmental authority is ordained by God. Therefore, whoever resists the governmental authority resists God's decree. Furthermore, we are convinced that we should seek the best for our country, that we should pray for our rulers, honor them, and speak respectfully about them, and that we should behave in an exemplary and blameless manner overall, in order to be a good witness for the Lord Jesus Christ. As Christians, therefore, we obey existing laws and ordinances not out of expediency, but out of conviction based on faith and obedience to God.

However, the Bible also teaches that governmental authority is not the highest authority, but rather – as the German Constitution also suggests, in its preamble – the almighty and eternal God, who at the end of time will judge all people, including those in authority, and either gift them with eternal life or punish them with eternal damnation. Therefore, our consciences are ultimately bound by the commandments of God. We are grateful that the

German Constitution also recognizes this and protects the freedom of faith and conscience of each individual from interference by the state in its Article 4, Paragraph 1, and thus binds the legislature, the executive power, and the judiciary.

Against this background, we are increasingly concerned about the development of the Corona policies and, in particular, the introduction of vaccine mandates for certain institutions and the announced introduction of general vaccine mandates. Although we are not against vaccinations per se, we would like to inform you that there are a large number of Christians in our country who cannot take the Corona vaccines for reasons of faith and conscience.

The reasons for this are manifold. For example, we share the view of many Christians that it is unethical to take vaccines that have been researched, manufactured, or tested using fetal cell lines, taken from the bodies of aborted children. Many Christians, moreover, are not convinced of the effectiveness and safety of the vaccines and therefore cannot in good conscience allow themselves to be given an injection that they fear may harm their God-given bodies. Since our bodies belong to God and not to the state, we must not simply submit to the state in certain matters concerning our bodies.

Even if you do not find these reasons convincing, we ask you nevertheless to acknowledge that a Christian cannot act against his conviction of faith and against his conscience; it is almost impossible for him, as the Reformer Dr. Martin Luther already said when he stood before the Diet of Worms to answer to the authorities, that his conscience is bound to the Holy Scriptures and "to do anything against conscience is neither safe nor salutary."

This applies to a Christian even if he is threatened with severe sanctions and even the loss of his job, his livelihood, his property, his freedom or his family; as again Dr. Martin Luther puts it in his world-famous hymn A Mighty Fortress is Our God, "Let goods and kindred go / this mortal life also / the body they may kill / God's truth abideth still / his kingdom is forever!"

If you decide to introduce general vaccine mandates, you will plunge thousands of Christian families in Germany into existential hardship, because they cannot comply with such an obligation for reasons of faith and conscience. Even if you were to ruin these families financially through fines and the loss of their jobs, they would still not be able to comply, because it is simply impossible for them to act against their conscience and thus sin against God.

Please be aware that this could possibly be perceived by some as persecution, because people would be punished by the state and ultimately forced to flee unless they are willing to act against their beliefs. We already know of many churches abroad, especially in the U.S., that look with dismay at developments in Germany in this regard.

The introduction of vaccine mandates for certain institutions will already lead to thousands of Christians losing their jobs. These are people who care especially sacrificially and devotedly for those in need, because they see in this not only a profession, but a divine calling and want to obey the Lord Jesus Christ, who says, "Love your neighbor as yourself."

We therefore appeal to you urgently not to enforce the existing vaccine mandates for certain institutions and to refrain from introducing general vaccine mandates or at least to provide for an exemption for people who refuse the vaccines for reasons of faith and conscience, as was the case, for example, with compulsory military service and as was already considered by the President of the Senate and Mayor Dr. Bovenschulte.

We ask you to consider our request and pray that Almighty God may bless you in your work. May God help us all.

Respectfully,

[Signatures][1]

---

[1] A complete list of all 120 signatories can be found at the Christian Corona Aid Working Group: https://acch.info/2022/02/17/schreiben-an-politiker/.

– Part 5 –

Looking Back on Two Years of Covid

Tobias Riemenschneider

Beloved brothers and sisters, it is a great privilege and joy for me to speak to you today, at this conference. The theme of the conference is "Churches in the Corona Crisis – Looking Back and Looking Forward," and I am speaking about looking back. In the next hour, we want to look at what has happened in the last two, soon to be two and a half years – especially with regard to the church. We want to understand why these things have happened, not superficially, but what the underlying spiritual realities are. We want to look at how the church, and we as Christians, should respond and what we need to learn from the last two years. For that is perhaps the greatest danger; that we have lived through and suffered through the last two years, but have learned nothing from them.

1. Historical Retrospect

So, I want to start by giving a brief overview of the restrictions on worship services over the last two years and the church's response to them. I think this look back is important, because I notice more and more often, in conversations, that people are already starting to forget what happened. Therefore, a brief refresher for our memory:

The first lockdown came in the spring of 2020. Worship services were completely prohibited throughout the country for several weeks. A nationwide, weeks-long, complete ban on religious services. To my knowledge, that is unprecedented in the history of our country. And it's astonishing that many today have already forgotten that. Live broadcasts were allowed, but many churches were not set up for that, and that is not an adequate substitute for an in-person service. I had never even heard the word "in-person service," before Corona, because a worship service is always an in-person service. That is, it is part of the essence of a worship service. Worship services are not celebrated by a pastor alone in front of a camera.

When church services were allowed again, other restrictions were introduced: social distancing, which meant that many churches no longer had enough space for everyone, so half of the members had to continue to stay at home. So, in many instances this still equated to a partial ban on church services. Social distancing also meant that one was not allowed to take the lonely and grieving and despairing in one's arms to comfort them, which would have been so urgently needed at this time. Then there were the mask mandates, prohibiting brethren from seeing their brother's face for months and years, neither his smile nor his sadness. Not to mention the other harmful effects of being forced to wear a mask for hours on end, even while singing. All this led to a situation where the brother, whom we are supposed to love so much that we are ready to lay down our lives for him, was suddenly perceived as a threat to our own lives by his mere existence, his mere presence: "Keep your distance! Wear a mask! Otherwise, the encounter with your brother could end fatally."

Depending on the state, there was a ban on the Lord's Supper, at least in the biblically transmitted form. Prohibition of baptisms, because you have to come close to baptize someone. In the case of a pastor friend from London, the police even broke up a service because he wanted to baptize. Our church baptized secretly, early in the morning in the cold, in a lonely lake. Then the prohibition, or at least severe restriction, of weddings and funerals. The ban on visiting the sick and dying. Then came the ban on singing. For more than half a year, the singing of God's praises was forbidden throughout the country – even longer in some states. I don't know if we realize what a sin it is to withhold praise from the Almighty Creator, who commands us to sing to Him. Those who can just accept this must ask themselves if they have even understood who God is! And a famous Bible teacher even dared to defend the ban on singing from a "biblical" point of view. Eventually, every church service had to be reported to the authorities in advance, and the data of all those attending the service had to be recorded and passed on to the authorities on request. This brought back very bad memories for brothers and sisters who still knew the GDR or the Soviet Union.

And so, the few faithful churches, which did not bow to injustice but obeyed God rather than men, had to worship for two years in constant fear of being discovered, betrayed, punished. For what reason? What was their crime? They were worshiping as the Lord commands and as He has been worshipped for 2,000 years. And in Canada, pastors were even jailed – along with criminals – for the very reason that they worshipped God.

But at least as grievous as the state abuses was the behavior of most churches in our country – and indeed around the world. Because the church imploded; it literally collapsed on itself. For the most part, people's immune systems were able to handle the virus. But the church's immune system against propaganda and against encroachment into worship proved to be non-existent. Most churches not only believed everything and went along with everything, but often it could not go fast and far enough for them. Many introduced measures that the state had not even ordered. This culminated in an action by the Protestant state church of Kurhessen-Waldeck, "Vaccinate your neighbor as yourself!" This is blasphemy, taking the holy commandment of God and trampling it into the dirt like this. But do not be deceived: God is not mocked! (Gal. 6:7).

And the brothers and sisters who did not want to participate in this injustice? They were often cast out of their own churches, and by their own shepherds. Those whose duty it was to protect the sheep from the attacks of the enemy began to harass and beat the sheep, to cast them out of the fold. The lies and hatred and segregation that we experienced in society found their way into the churches and among brothers and sisters as well. No immune system. Just total conformity to the world.

During this time, countless brothers and sisters from other churches visited our church. And, with tears, they told how they had suffered. What their own shepherds had done to them. And I heard unbelievable stories. What I have not heard is that even one of these pastors repented. Those brothers and sisters suffered a lot. There were people in our church service who started crying just because they saw a friendly face again after months, or because a hand was extended to them, or they were allowed to sing. Regardless of how one assesses the risk of Covid – how much additional suffering was caused by the restrictions and the reactions of the churches!

And while some shepherds, good and faithful servants of their Lord, put themselves in the front line, where the bullets flew around their ears, to fight for their Lord and for their sheep, and while some of them sat in prison for this, some hirelings sat in their armchairs at home and wrote attacks and slander against these brothers. King Ahab had come to steal Naboth's vineyard. And these men accused Naboth: what was he thinking of, to defy the king! In Germany, two gentlemen in particular are among these slanderers; and it is a shame that their churches did not take action against them.

And even though the situation I have just described was by far the biggest problem, there was also the opposite problem. There was also a backlash that swung too far, and some drove into the ditch on the other side of the road. One well-known pastor declared that submission to the state, as Scripture teaches in Romans 13, simply would not apply in our democracy. This is a false and unbiblical radicalism. Another shut down his church permanently because he thought that the age of the church was now over forever. From now on, they could only meet in small groups underground. He surrendered without a fight; he laid down his arms without having fired even a single shot. These were overreactions that were perhaps understandable because of the great pressure we were under, but which were nevertheless wrong and unbiblical.

So much for a look back at what has happened in the last two years in relation to the church of Christ. And we should not forget what has happened! We should not forget the fear and the pressure and the suffering we had. But we don't just want to remember what happened, we want to understand *why* it happened – and why it can happen again.

2. Why did this happen?

Why did these measures of the state come about, these encroachments into the church but also into all areas of life, into work and family and personal relationships and, with mask and vaccine mandates, even into one's own body? By that I don't mean who is pursuing what interests and who is pulling the strings and what is the role of the WHO and the WEF and of Bill Gates and Klaus Schwab. Those who want to look into this may do so, but for me it is enough to know: Yes, the whole world lies in the power of the evil one, and there are evil people who plan evil things, and they also join together to carry out their evil plans. But I am not so much interested in that. Rather, I want us to understand what spiritual realities are behind this. Because the actors may change. But the spiritual realities behind them will probably continue to concern us, in various forms, for a long time.

The first thing we have to understand if we want to have a biblical worldview, if we want to understand biblically what is happening in our world right now, is that there is no neutrality towards God. Neutrality is a myth. There are only two kinds of people: those who have been justified by grace through faith in the Lord Jesus Christ and His atoning blood and who are now children of God, and those who are children of the devil. There is nothing in between. There is no neutrality in spiritual matters. This is the teaching of Scripture: either you are for Christ, or you are against Him; either you are righteous or lawless, you are light or darkness, you belong to Christ or to Belial, you are a believer or an unbeliever, you are the temple of God or of idols (2 Cor. 6:14-16). And the unbelievers, the wicked, the children of the devil, they are characterized by being like their father and wanting to do their father's desires. And he is a murderer and a liar and the father of lies (John 8:44). The granny next door may be ever so friendly – if she does not believe in the risen Lord, then she is an enemy of God, she is darkness and a child of the devil.

This is something that many Christians do not understand: There is no neutrality in spiritual matters. And that is why there is no neutral chancellor and no neutral minister of health and no neutral state. They all have a religion, they all serve a god, and if it is not the Christian religion and the triune God of Scripture, then it is a demonic religion and a demonic idol. If they do not love God, then they are not neutral toward Him but they hate Him. And if they do not serve God, they serve an idol. And the result of this is always lies and hatred and death; for all who hate God love death (Prov. 8:36).

This does not mean that the state, and the people who govern it, do nothing but evil and do nothing at all that is objectively good. What it does mean is that the godless ideology of the state will always show in its actions. And, for the first time, we have really experienced this in the last two years. Our state was once Christianized. Christianity was once so widespread that the thinking of those in authority was also influenced by Christian values, by the law of God, which determines, for all people at all times, what is good and evil, right and wrong. And that was reflected, for example, in our constitution. The people who wrote our constitution knew that people are sinners and will abuse their power. They were still vividly aware of this after the Third Reich. That is why there is separation of powers, and that is why there are constitutional rights as defensive rights of citizens against the state.

But in the end, it's all just ink on paper. If no one adheres to the constitution anymore, or if it is reinterpreted at will, then it is all worthless. John Adams, Founding Father and second President of the USA, already knew that. He wrote about the American Constitution, which is not unlike ours, "Our Constitution was made only for a moral and religious people. It is wholly inadequate to the government of any other." And by "religious" he meant Christianity at that time, of course, because he himself came from a Puritan home.

Unfortunately, this is no longer true of our people. We are no longer a Christian nation; we are no longer a moral nation, because in recent decades our country has become de-Christianized. This development had begun much earlier, centuries ago, with the Enlightenment and with Rousseau, and then it got a rocket boost from Darwin, but in the last decades the de-Christianization of Germany has been almost completed. The new worldview that dominates the thinking of most people, and also of those in authority, is no longer the Christian worldview, with its belief in a Creator God who has given a good and just law according to which He will judge us, but materialism and radical naturalism, *i.e.*, the idea that reality arose from an impersonal origin and evolved into its present form through impersonal mutations – without God and without transcendent meaning and purpose.

And such a worldview is not without consequences for the thinking and actions of people and the state. It has an impact on moral concepts and on the laws that are enacted. Francis Schaeffer foresaw this more than 40 years ago. He wrote that this new worldview would displace the Christian worldview, both in the beliefs of individuals and in its cultural impact. And because these two worldviews are completely antithetical to each other, in content and moral consequences, they would lead to very different social developments and decisions by governments, which would result in the drafting and introduction of new laws. This is exactly what has happened. The ungodly have successfully done what they announced 60 years ago: they have made the "march through the institutions." The culture is de-Christianized; the schools are de-Christianized; and so are the rulers, the state and all its institutions de-Christianized. We now live in an ungodly state that is governed by ungodly people. And this has an impact on the morals and the laws that the state enacts, which increasingly call evil good and good evil.

But many Christians do not understand this. In the last two years, they have believed that the state is spiritually neutral and that we can certainly believe its propaganda and trust its narratives for it will surely tell us the truth, it will surely not lie to us! But we are talking about the very state that denies basic truths of creation that every child knows; that denies that there are two genders, that marriage is between a man and a woman, that children have a father and a mother, yes, that denies even the Creator Himself and teaches the children that the whole cosmos was created by a big bang, when billions of years ago nothing exploded, and that man was only a cosmic accident, stardust, a bag of mostly water, in whose brains a few neurons fire at random, without ultimate meaning, without transcendent purpose. It is the very state that hates God so much that it fights against all divine truths. And because it cannot reach God Himself, it fights that which is most like God, namely the image of God in man as created by a God and not as a mere byproduct of chance. This very state, which has proven itself to be such a liar, a child of the devil, is blindly trusted by many Christians when it says, "There is a serious disease and, for your own protection, I must take away your constitutional rights and intrude on your worship!"

But they not only blindly trust the state, they even believe that the state really only wants our best; that it only wants to protect us, that it only wants to save lives. "Isn't that a good concern? You should be lenient if the state oversteps the mark a bit, because its concern is a good one!" Do they actually know which state they are talking about? They are talking about the very state that allows and promotes that 100,000 babies every year are ripped to shreds in their mothers' wombs, in unimaginably cruel ways. They are talking about the very state that now gives children the right to be mutilated by a "sex-change surgery" in such a way that they will never be able to have children themselves. They are talking about the very state that promotes homosexual unions, from which life can never come forth. They are talking about the very state that is thinking about ending the lives of the elderly and the sick by euthanasia. And all this under the guise of mercy and love of neighbor. This very state should now all of a sudden be so concerned about our lives – especially the lives of the old and the sick? Do not be fooled by the myth of neutrality!

Sadly, the church is also partly to blame for this development, this de-Christianization of society and the state. The Protestant state church, like the state, is itself de-Christianized; as are many independent churches, where people have become completely liberal, no longer believing and teaching the Bible, and where it's primarily about my feelings and my entertainment. Dear ones, if any of you are still in one of these churches, what are you doing there? What fellowship does light have with darkness? "Come out of her, my people, lest you take part in her sins, lest you share in her" (Rev. 18:4). And the few Bible-believing churches? They are mostly pietistic. They have withdrawn, concentrated on themselves, formed enclaves, and limited Christ's kingdom to their own hearts and their church. They have noticed that the state is becoming more and more evil and godless, but their reaction has not been to fight against this, but to withdraw, to encapsulate themselves.

And so, the church no longer exercises its office as a prophetic voice in this world. It no longer boldly proclaims God's Word to all people, including those in authority. And thus, she is no longer light and salt for the world. It is the church's task to proclaim, "Now therefore, O kings, be wise; be warned, O rulers of the earth. Serve the Lord with fear, and rejoice with trembling. Kiss the Son, lest he be angry, and you perish in the way, for His wrath is quickly kindled" (Ps. 2:10-12). But the church has not done that, has no longer sounded its prophetic voice in this country. Today, when someone preaches about political issues and addresses those in authority, he must expect criticism from his own ranks, because this is considered unspiritual. "The church has to stay out of such matters!" As if the Word of God does not apply to all people! As if His commandments do not demand obedience from all! As if He is not the God and Judge of all! As if He is not the great King over the whole earth, the King of kings and the Lord of lords!

And so, the evil in the world was no longer resisted with the Word, and the world sank deeper and deeper into the bosom of the evil one and became more and more hostile to God. What could the churches have done decades ago, when still 95% of Germans were members of a church! If they had fought with all their might against feminism and fornication and abortion; if they had excommunicated politicians who supported these things and publicly denounced their injustice and opposed it with the Word of God, so that they would not have been re-elected. But the churches did not want to wage the battle out there. And so, the world has become so hostile to God that it is now taking the battle into the churches. Because remember, there is no neutrality.

When the countries of the Soviet Union or the GDR were de-Christianized, the result was not a neutral state that simply let Christians live their faith in peace. The result was a dictatorship, a totalitarian state that monitored all people and intervened in all areas of life in order to impose its state ideology, its state religion. For if the state no longer believes that there is a God above it, to whom even those who govern must answer, then the state itself becomes God. For there is no higher power, no higher authority on this earth than the state. The state is legislator and judge and executioner in one person. It dictates what people are allowed to do and say and even think, and it punishes the dissenters. It also has the power of the police and the military, which no citizen can resist. And so, the state itself becomes God, the supreme moral authority, which determines what is good and evil and demands absolute obedience from its citizens. It becomes increasingly totalitarian, penetrating all areas of life like a cancer. We witness a growing statism, an absolute state rule over all spheres of life, as in socialism or communism. And anyone who does not comply is publicly scorned, silenced, cancelled on social media, re-educated through media indoctrination, made compliant through social pressure and threats of severe consequences, such as losing their jobs or having their children taken away, and in the end locked away. For they are heretics, enemies of the state, and inciters of the people.

We have seen the beginnings of this statism, this totalitarian rule of the state, in the last two years. And how quickly it happened! But we should have known it would happen. Because the state has been harboring fantasies of omnipotence for a long time. I only call to mind the statement of one Social Democratic Party politician who, 20 years ago, was already pushing for the radical expansion of daycare places and all-day schools saying, "We want to have air supremacy over the cribs." The man who said this, back then, is now the German Chancellor. This should give us all chills. This is pure state totalitarianism: The state wants to take the children, and as early as possible, to indoctrinate them according to its godless ideology. And, dear parents, think carefully whether you want to entrust the education of your children to this state, in day-care centers and state schools.

But the state has a problem, because it cannot simply introduce a new state religion without selling it well to the people. The people must believe that this new religion is really good and necessary. And just as every religion has its priests to mediate between its god and the people, the state religion also needs priests to communicate the new religion to the people. And it finds them in science, in so-called experts. For who wants to say something against science? He must be a fool! Who wants to say something against experts! You perhaps? You have no right to do so, because you are not an expert yourself! The experts must be believed – of course, only the selected ones who actually proclaim that which corresponds to the state ideology. And if you don't believe them, then you are a science denier – and one can hardly be much worse.

This, too, we have seen in the last two years more than ever before, the rise of scientism, *i.e.*, the belief that scientific knowledge should govern all human actions, including in politics. But this leads to the inhumane results that we have witnessed in the last two years: A virologist tells us what we should do to contain a virus – and then we do it all, regardless of the harm and suffering it causes to many people, so long as there is a scientific justification for the measures that we take. C.S. Lewis had recognized this early on. He wrote as early as 1958, "Again, the new oligarchy must more and more base its claim to plan us on its claim to knowledge. If we are to be mothered, mother must know best. This means they must increasingly rely on the advice of scientists, till in the end the politicians proper become merely the scientists' puppets. Technocracy is the form to which a planned society must tend. Now I dread specialists in power because they are specialists speaking outside their special subjects. Let scientists tell us about sciences. But government involves questions about the good for man, and justice, and what things are worth having at what price; and on these a scientific training gives a man's opinion no added value. Let the doctor tell me I shall die unless I do so-and-so; but whether life is worth having on those terms is no more a question for him than for any other man." We see these things being fulfilled before our very eyes. How the state of Romans 13, which is supposed to be God's servant by praising good and punishing evil, becomes the state of Revelation 13, the beast that blasphemes God and wants all worship for himself and persecutes Christians by praising evil and punishing good.

These are the spiritual realities that are behind the last two years and that will continue to trouble us in one form or another in the future, be it a pandemic, be it sexuality and transgenderism, be it family and the air supremacy over the cribs, be it the climate or whatever else may come. The state has its own religion that determines its actions, and this is anti-God and anti-Christian – and we will continue to experience this in the future. In the behavior of the state and in the laws it enacts, it will become apparent, time and again, that the state is hostile to God and anti-Christian. And this will not remain without consequences for us Christians and for our worship services and for what we are still allowed to think and say and do. Life in this new world will not be easy for those who want to remain faithful to the Lord. The good news is that this worldview cannot last. It is so contrary to all reason, to all truth, that, sooner or later, it must collapse. It cannot last, because we all live in God's world, and any ideology that so blatantly goes against God must perish. But it may be decades before it collapses. And until then, it can cause much suffering and much persecution for us Christians.

3. What Should the Christian Response be?

This question can be answered more easily as of today. Because today, here at this conference, a declaration will be presented to the world. And because it is being presented here in Frankfurt, it has a fitting title. I hold here in my hands the FRANKFURT DECLARATION OF CHRISTIAN AND CIVIL LIBERTIES. This declaration has been penned by pastors from various continents, over the past year and a half. It already carries the signatures of dozens of faithful pastors from America, Europe, Africa, and Australia, among them names like Dr. John MacArthur, Dr. Voddie Baucham, Dr. James White, Dr. Joe Boot, Douglas Wilson, Phil Johnson, Geoff Thomas, Tim Conway, Jeff Durbin, Joel Webbon, Josh Buice, Justin Peters, Jacob Reaume, Tim Stephens, Dr. James Coates, and many others. This is our response to what has happened in the last two years. We hereby oppose the abuse of power and the totalitarianism of the state. So, what does this declaration state?

ARTICLE 1: GOD THE CREATOR AS SOVEREIGN LAWGIVER AND JUDGE

We deny that the state has the right to define what morality is, and to demand obedience from its citizens when this is contrary to God's commandments. Why? Because not the state, but God alone has the right to determine what is good and evil, and because He will judge all people accordingly. And because secular humanism and the relativistic ethics of the state have no transcendent basis for morality and therefore cannot be binding.

ARTICLE 2: GOD AS THE SOURCE OF TRUTH AND THE ROLE OF SCIENCE

We reject the notion that human governments are morally and ideologically neutral and that their narratives should be believed unconditionally, as if they always told the truth. We oppose fear-mongering and propaganda and indoctrination, scientism and science that abandons the scientific method and ignores and suppresses objections from dissenting voices. Why? Because God is the Truth, but all men are liars. And because human science has limits and must not put itself in God's place by pretending to be omniscient like God.

ARTICLE 3: MANKIND AS THE IMAGE OF GOD

We reject all degrading acts of a state through manipulation and intimidation, mandating medical treatments, or restricting God-given personal freedoms. We oppose vaccine passports, social distancing, and mask-wearing as a requirement for access to public places or participation in work or social life. We oppose the criminalization, exclusion, occupational discrimination, and other deprivation of rights of people who do not comply with such orders. And we reject developments towards transhumanism and the technological surveillance and control of people. Why? Because God created man in His image, and therefore man has dignity and God-given, inalienable rights and liberties that no state may take away from him. These rights and liberties include the right to visit the sick and comfort the dying, to attend funerals, to witness the birth of one's child, to marry in a public ceremony, to fellowship and feast together, and to engage in respectable work, as well as the right to make one's own medical decisions.

ARTICLE 4: GOD-GIVEN MANDATES AND LIMITS OF AUTHORITY

We reject totalitarian ideologies of governments that do not recognize the limits of their authority and encroach on the church or the family. We reject the tendencies of governments to centralize the beliefs and behavior of their citizens by creating an authoritarian society in which the state is absolute and silences and re-educates those who dissent. And we especially oppose the notion that children are the property of the state and that the state is allowed to indoctrinate them as if God had given them to the state and not to their parents. Why? Because all earthly authorities derive their authority from God, who is above all and to whom all must give an account. He has established their different spheres of authority and thus set limits to their authority. God has given the state the authority to praise good and punish evil, thereby protecting the God-given rights and liberties of people. He has given the church the authority to make disciples of all nations through the preaching of the gospel and to establish and govern churches under the headship of Christ. And He has given the family the authority to promote social cohesion and sexual fidelity, and to protect, care for, teach, and raise children in the ways of the Lord. And we, as citizens, parents and Christians, do not allow the state to interfere in the areas that God has placed under our sole responsibility, because it would be sinful to abdicate our God-given responsibility.

ARTICLE 5: CHRIST AS THE HEAD OF THE CHURCH

We reject the notion that the state has authority over the church to regulate its affairs in matters of faith and practice or to reduce its activities to a non-essential status. We believe in the functional separation of church and state. We therefore reject all measures of the state that impose coercive measures on the church and criminalize, hinder, or regulate its activities, which are carried out as a service to its Lord. Why? Because the state is not above the church, but the church belongs to the Lord Jesus Christ alone, for He purchased it with His blood, and we are accountable to Him alone in all matters of faith and practice. We give to Caesar what is Caesar's, but we will be zealous to also give to God what is God's.

So, for all of you who have been waiting for a response by the church: Here it is. This declaration is intended to help Christians to be able to reason and argue on the basis of God's Word. And it is meant as a statement to the state, so it knows where the church stands. The German chancellor says there are no more red lines for him? Herewith we draw the red line!

4. What Should we Learn from Corona?

Let's conclude by asking what we should learn from the last two years. I would like to briefly mention four points:

A) biblical worldview

Develop a biblical worldview. Let your thinking be changed more and more by God's word, so that you do not think like the world and are not conformed to the world. Understand that there is no spiritual neutrality, but that you are in spiritual warfare. The state and the people who govern it always have an ideology, always have a religion, and if it is not Christian, it is anti-Christian. Therefore, don't just believe everything the state says, and don't just do everything the state says, but examine it. You also examine what your pastor says. Then examine even more what the godless state says. And if what the state says turns out to be a lie, then don't go along with that lie. As the Russian writer Aleksandr Solzhenitsyn put it, 'Live Not by Lies.'

B) BIBLICAL ECCLESIOLOGY

Develop a biblical ecclesiology, a biblical doctrine of the church! Every Christian needs a church. You can't live on livestreams. You need a pastor who knows you; you need brothers and sisters who know you. Especially in the times ahead, you need encouragement and exhortation to faithfulness from them. And that's what the pastor whose livestream you're watching would tell you too, at least if he's a good pastor. And although this may anger some of you, don't believe the people who say you can only gather in house groups now. I understand if someone is disappointed with the churches. But a house group as a permanent solution is not biblical. I am not saying anything against a house church in the sense of a normal, biblically ordered church, if possible, with an ordained pastor, which is just so small that it meets in houses. That is biblical. But the Bible only knows churches, not any other groups as a substitute for churches. Therefore, house groups should strive to become real (house) churches.

Watch carefully which church you join. It is not enough for a church to have a doctrine that is faithful to the Bible. It must also demonstrate this faithfulness in its behavior. So, ask how this church has behaved in the last two years. Has it been faithful and courageous? Or is it only faithful as long as the state does not object, but collapses as soon as the state comes against it? These are crucial questions, because in the future we will increasingly have to distinguish a faithful from an apostate church by how it behaves toward the anti-Christian state. Does it submit to all state intervention? Does it believe every state narrative? Or does it resist biblically, even if this should result in persecution? Therefore, find a hill you can defend, a church with faithful brothers and sisters and courageous pastors who will fight alongside you and who will continue to be faithful in the future because they have proven to be faithful in the last two years. And if there is no such church near you, move! Seek first the kingdom of God, be ready to leave everything and everyone to follow Christ! He promises that He will bless you a hundredfold.

And if you are in a church that has gone along with everything for the last two years, if you have a shepherd who has been weak and cowardly, who has not protected the sheep, but has harassed and beaten them and cast them out, and if he has not repented of it – then please leave that church. Do not stay under such a shepherd, for he has proved to be a hireling. Or do you think something like Corona could never happen again? Do you think your pastor will react differently then? If you stay in such a church, if you stay under such a hireling, then you have not learned from Corona. If you learn only one thing from Corona, let it be that you need a faithful church with courageous shepherds.

C) BIBLICAL RESISTANCE THEOLOGY

Develop a biblical resistance theology. We must obey God rather than men, even if that results in persecution. Some have justified their passivity in the last two years by saying that the state interference was not persecution. If there were persecution, then they would resist and obey God rather than men. But it doesn't work that way. You don't obey God rather than men only when persecution comes. You obey God rather than men, and that is precisely why persecution comes. Because you obey God rather than the state, the state will persecute you, not the other way around.

When the state performs its duty as God's servant by praising good and punishing evil, we joyfully submit to it. But when the state puts itself in the place of God and makes itself the highest moral authority, imposing godless ideologies and calling evil good and good evil, when it demands of us something that is sin in the eyes of God, then we must resist. And when the state acts as a totalitarian tyrant, encroaching on the spheres of authority that God has given to the church or to the family or to the individual, we must resist. As the great, Scottish reformer, John Knox, said, "Resistance to tyranny is obedience to God." And it is equally true the other way around: no resistance to tyranny is disobedience to God.

In concrete terms, this means that when the state forbids worship, we resist, because God has commanded worship. If the state forbids singing to God, we resist, because God has commanded singing to Him. If the state forbids or regulates baptisms or the Lord's Supper, we resist because God commands to baptize and to celebrate the Lord's Supper. When the state commands that distance be kept between brothers and sisters, we resist because God has commanded that we love one another and not treat one another as a mortal threat. When the state dictates that only people who are tested or vaccinated or wear a mask may worship, we resist because Christ invites all who labor and are heavy laden. And if our resistance means suffering persecution because of it, then we want to suffer it gladly. And we want to stand by those who also suffer because they obey God rather than men.

D) BIBLICAL CHRISTOLOGY AND ESCHATOLOGY

Develop a biblical Christology and eschatology. In the last two years I have heard again and again from Christians that it is all over now, now the great tribulation begins, and Christ will come and rapture His church next Tuesday. And these people then sank into passivity and lethargy. They did nothing against the injustice. They simply gave up. Just like the pastor who closed his church because now the end times had begun, and the time of the church was over. Regardless of which eschatological view you hold, if it leads to such results, then something is off. It is not your job to puzzle over the time when Christ will return. It is your job to faithfully work for Him and testify of Him until He returns.

And you can do so joyfully and confidently despite all dangers and even in the face of an overpowering state. For Christ is Lord over the whole earth and over all people, and even the most powerful states can do nothing against Him. When the kings and the nations rise up and rage against Him, He can only mock them, so futile and ridiculous is their rebellion. Develop a biblical view of Christ as the risen and ascended King. Do not have your eyes anxiously fixed on the mighty state, but fix your eyes on the mighty Lord, who is above all. He is also Lord over the chancellor and the minister of health. All power has been given to Him in heaven and on earth. And therefore, take courage and fight the good fight. Do not sink into pessimism and passivity, do not retreat, but joyfully fight the fight that the Lord has set before you.

Especially addressed to the pastors: Let the prophetic voice of the church resound boldly and clearly in our land again. Preach the word in season and out of season. Preach against ungodliness and unrighteousness. Preach against the wicked schemes of the politicians. Proclaim that Christ is lord over all. And if that means witnessing for Christ in a time that is much more difficult and hostile to God than the decades before, then so be it. This whole godless ideology will collapse. And when that happens, we need faithful Christians who are instructed in a biblical worldview, who have been taught to observe all that Christ has commanded us, so that they will be able to rebuild this country according to biblical standards. May the Lord strengthen us, and may His grace be with us all. To Him be glory and eternal dominion. Amen.

– Part 6 –

Frankfurt Declaration of Christian and Civil Liberties

Dr. Paul Hartwig, Steven Lloyd, and Tobias Riemenschneider

In the course of human events, it sometimes becomes necessary for people of good faith to speak out against the abuse of power. This should be done only after serious and prayerful deliberation, and even then, in an attitude of humility and with respect for the authorities that have been established by God. Such protest should be expressed in the hope that civil authorities who are found to be eroding rights and liberties may yet fulfill their responsibility as their rightful guardians.

A few concerned pastors from different continents, moved by an emergent totalitarianism of the state over all realms of society, and particularly the church, and the disregard of God-given and constitutionally guaranteed rights during the Covid crisis, joined in common cause to craft a solemn declaration, which seeks to address these threats with the timeless truths of God's Word. The following affirmations and denials, derived from biblical principles, we put forth for consideration by all Christians and relevant authorities, in the hope that this document *will give light and strength for faithful witness to Jesus Christ in our day.*

2 Sam. 12:1-14; Acts 4:24-29; Rom. 13:1-7; 1 Pet. 2:13-14

Article 1: God the Creator as Sovereign Lawgiver and Judge

We affirm that the Triune God – Father, Son, and Holy Spirit – is the personal Creator of all things visible and invisible, the blessed and only Sovereign, and the ultimate Lawgiver for all human conduct. We believe that He has revealed in the Holy Scriptures and the conscience of men an unchangeable morality which is rooted in His own character, and which defines the nature of good and evil conduct for all people at all times. As the Lawgiver, God has appointed a day on which He will judge the world in righteousness by a man, the risen Lord Jesus Christ. To him be honor and eternal dominion. Amen.

We therefore deny that impersonal matter is the final reality behind all things and the belief that human conduct is merely a biological or sociological phenomenon. Since God is the ultimate Lawgiver and Judge, we deny the right of any earthly authority to define morality and require unconditional obedience of their citizens when contrary to His law. We also have good grounds to question the modern state's ethical pronouncements and moral vision since their secular humanism and relativistic ethics have no transcendent basis for human behavior or morality.

Gen. 1:1; 2:15-17; Ex. 1:17; 20:1-17; Josh. 2:3-6; Ps. 9:7-8; Dan. 6:11; Mic. 6:8; Matt. 28:19; Acts 4:19; 5:29; 9:25; 12:17; 17:31; Rom. 1:32; 2:14-16; 11:36; Col. 1:16; 1 Tim. 1:17; 6:15-16; 2 Tim. 3:16-17; Heb. 11:3; James 4:12; Rev. 4:11

Article 2: God as the Source of Truth and the Role of Science

We affirm that God, the Creator, is the Truth and that therefore objective truth exists and can be derived from His revelation in Scripture and nature, and from any facts which can be credibly verified. We endorse science which seeks to discover, through the scientific method and debate, the truths that God has built into the natural world. We also affirm the limitations of science, including its inability to speak authoritatively on areas outside its purview and its propensity to err when data is lacking. Since man has fallen into sin, we further affirm that all his thoughts, deductions, and institutions contain degrees of corruption which tend to distort, manipulate, or suppress the truth.

We therefore deny that human governments are morally and ideologically neutral and always know or seek what is good for their citizens and that their narrative should be unconditionally trusted. We reject any deception, fearmongering, propagandizing, and indoctrination by the state and mass media, and all reporting on critical world issues which is premature, selective, or ideologically manipulative. We further reject the assertions of any so-called "scientific consensus" which abandons the scientific method and ignores or suppresses the concerns of dissident voices. We likewise reject scientism since, even when scientific findings correctly describe a particular phenomenon, they cannot adequately and normatively address complex social realities or prescribe policies that have ethical implications.

Gen. 6:5; Ps. 19:1-8; 31:6; 119:160; Eccles. 7:29; John 3:33; 14:6; 16:13; 17:17; Rom. 1:18-20; 2 Cor. 4:2; Eph. 2:3;

1 Tim. 3:15; 2 Tim. 3:16-17; James 2:9; Rev. 13:11-15

Article 3: Mankind as the Image of God

We affirm that every human being is created in the image and likeness of God (*imago Dei*) and therefore has inherent dignity and worth, along with certain inalienable rights and liberties requisite for a proper human life. These rights and liberties include the right to corporate worship, personal and in-person relationships, vocational employments, and participation in the important events of human life such as the right to comfort the sick and the dying (especially of one's own family), to attend funerals, to witness the birth of one's child, to marry in a public gathering, to fellowship and eat together with others, and to engage in honorable work. We also affirm that governments should recognize that each individual is responsible for their own bodily well-being and should protect the right to personal medical self-determination.

We therefore deny the dehumanizing actions of a governmental authority or any other institution to subject any person to psychological manipulation and intimidation. This includes fostering suspicion of others by portraying them as potential threats to the common and individual good. We likewise oppose the state's mandating of medical decisions for its citizens, and the criminalizing, enforced segregation, vocational disempowerment, and any other deprivation of rights of persons who choose not to comply with their government's medical policies. We thus reject all forms of medical coercion and any restrictions on individual freedoms for people who are not infected with any contagious, life-threatening disease; this includes the implementation of vaccine passes, social distancing, or mask-wearing as a general prerequisite for access to public places or for participation in work or social life. Global trends toward transhumanism and technological surveillance and control over human beings we also oppose since they undermine the human agency which is so fundamental to our God-given calling to live as His image bearers.

Gen. 1:26-28; 2:24; 9:6; Ex. 20:9; Dan. 3:1-30; Matt. 25:31-40; 1 Cor. 6:12-20; 1 Thess. 4:11-12; James 3:9; 5:14-15; Rev. 13:16-17

Article 4: God-given Mandates and Limits of Authority

We affirm that all earthly authorities derive their authority ('the right to be obeyed') from God, who is over all and to whom all must give account. We believe that He has established their different spheres of responsibility (*i.e.*, mandates) and in so doing has set limits to their authority. God has delegated authority to civil governments for the purpose of rewarding good and punishing evil, and to protect the God-given rights and freedoms granted to all people. He has also delegated authority to the church in its various expressions, particularly to make disciples of all nations by preaching the Word of God, and to establish and administer redeemed communities of faith living under the authority of Christ. In addition, He has delegated authority to the family as the basic unit of society for the purpose of fostering societal cohesion and sexual fidelity, and to protect, provide for, raise, and educate children in the way of the Lord. We affirm our right as citizens, parents, and Christians to freely self-determine our beliefs and behaviors based on these truths.

We therefore deny totalitarian ideologies of governments which do not recognize the boundaries of their authority and usurp the authority delegated by God to the church or the family. In particular, we reject the tendency of governments to centralize beliefs and conduct for their citizens by creating an authoritarian society in which the state is absolute. Such totalitarianism and statism is built upon beliefs that have fundamentally redefined good and evil and the nature of human beings, and are contrary to the divine order of things. The effect of such beliefs is to enslave individual and religious freedoms, and engender an ideological intolerance which seeks to silence, cancel, and re-educate those who disagree. We also oppose the view that children are the property of the state and therefore subjects to be indoctrinated, and also any encouragement or manipulation of children to undergo medical procedures without parental consent.

Deut. 6:6-7; Matt. 22:20-21; 28:18-19; John 17:14; Rom. 12:1-2; 13:1-7; Eph. 5:21-6:4; Phil. 2:14-16; Col. 3:18-20; 1 Tim. 2:1-2; Heb. 13:17; 1 Pet. 2:13-14; 4:15; Rev. 13:7-8

Article 5: Christ as the Head of the Church

We affirm that the church of the Lord Jesus Christ belongs to Him at the cost of His life and that it is accountable to Him alone in all matters of faith and practice. We believe that Christ's command to give to Caesar (*i.e.*, the civil authority) what belongs to Caesar and to God what belongs to God establishes the functional independence of the church from the state. We believe that Christ, who is Lord over all, calls all without distinction of any kind to freely and regularly gather together in His Name in local congregations to seek and serve Him in truth and love. We further affirm that the activities of the local church insofar as they are essential acts of worship are to be regulated by Christ alone.

We therefore deny that any other authority has jurisdiction over the church to regulate any of its affairs in matters of faith and practice, or to relegate its activities to a non-essential status. We thus repudiate all actions of the state that impose coercive measures over the church and criminalize, inhibit, or regulate any of its activities which are undertaken as acts of service toward its Lord. Lastly, we resist the trend of digital platforms in Christian worship and ministry to become substitutes for congregational and in-person ministry which are essential to our faith.

Matt. 18:20; 22:21; Acts 5:28-29; 10:36; 20:28; Rom. 13:6-7; 1 Cor. 12:12-13; 2 Cor. 4:5; 5:10; Eph. 1:20b-23; 3:20; 4:15-16; Col. 1:27; 1 Tim. 6:3-5; Heb. 10:24-25; Rev. 5:9

A CALL FOR RESPECT, REPENTANCE, AND RESISTANCE

We commend and express our gratitude to those civil authorities who respect the essential nature of these Christian beliefs and practices and who have a high regard for individual and religious freedoms. To those civil authorities who have disregarded these freedoms, we call on you to repent and to become again the protectors of liberty and of the rights that God has given to all men, lest in the abuse of your God-given authority, you become liable to God's wrath. To those who desire to compel us to obey the secular state rather than God, we respectfully, but firmly say (like the three Hebrews who refused to worship Nebuchadnezzar's golden statue), "We have no need to answer you in this matter. The God we serve is able to save us from you, and He will rescue us from your hand. But even if He does not, we want you to know that we will not serve your gods or worship the idols you have set up." (*Dan. 3:16-18*)

To our brothers and sisters in Christ around the world we say, "Be strong and courageous. Do not be frightened, and do not be dismayed, for the Lord your God is with you wherever you go." (*Josh.1:9*) It appears that the world may well be entering a time of testing, not only for the church, but for everyone who believes in freedom and who opposes tyranny. Let us stand with those who are hard-pressed, arrested, or forcefully isolated because they have chosen to do what is right. Let us stand in solidarity with those whose churches are forcefully closed or who are exiled from their congregations. Let us help and support in practical ways those who are fined or have to forfeit their employment for the sake of Christ. And we ask our brothers and sisters who have lived under persecution all their lives to pray for us, that God would give us the grace to bless those who persecute us and to pray for them; that God would give us the courage to stand firm in our faith as His witnesses; and that He, who is Lord over all, would give us the strength to remain faithful and persevere to the end. Amen.

2 Sam. 12:1-14; Dan. 5:22-23; Matt. 24:12-13; 1 Cor. 16:13-14; Eph. 5:10-13

* * *

[Signatures][1]

---

1 A complete list of all 50 initial signers and all further signers can be found at The Frankfurt Declaration of Christian & Civil Liberties https://frankfurtdeclaration.com.

– PART 7 –

'CHRISTIANS AGAINST THE ABUSE OF POWER': THEOLOGIANS AROUND THE WORLD SIGN STATEMENT REJECTING GOVERNMENT LOCKDOWNS[1]

Ben Zeisloft

"The city of men failed at Babel, and it will fail again today."

THIRTEEN CENTURIES AGO, an Anglo-Saxon missionary named Boniface destroyed an oak tree in Germania considered sacred to Thor, leading many locals to redirect their worship toward the Triune God. Today, pastors from around the world are likewise converging upon Germany to do battle with the idols of our age.

Last week, the Frankfurt Declaration of Christian and Civil Liberties was published in response to the authoritarian spirit gripping many Western governments. In a series of interviews with *The Daily Wire*, several of the signatories – many of whom have already gained international attention for their righteous resistance to unlawful totalitarianism – explained how Christianity is the only basis by which mankind may reject the abuse of power.

---

1   The article was first published by The Daily Wire at https://www.dailywire.com/news/christians-against-the-abuse-of-power-theologians-around-the-world-sign-statement-rejecting-government-lockdowns.

God the Creator

In the Western world, materialism – the argument that matter and motion are the full extent of reality – has led to a denial of God as sovereign Creator. The Frankfurt Declaration affirms the role of God as the ultimate source of truth and ethics.

We believe that He has revealed in the Holy Scriptures and the conscience of men an unchangeable morality which is rooted in His own character, and which defines the nature of good and evil conduct for all people at all times. As the Lawgiver, God has appointed a day on which He will judge the world in righteousness by a man, the risen Lord Jesus Christ. To him be honor and eternal dominion. Amen.

The statement therefore denies the notion that any earthly authority is able to define morality or mandate disobedience to what God has prescribed – especially as many governments embrace postmodernism, which is incapable of providing a coherent basis for morality.

Dr. Joe Boot – founder of the Ezra Institute for Contemporary Christianity in Ontario, Canada – told *The Daily Wire* that the Christian notion of a "cosmos that is distinct from, yet governed by an infinite personal God who is always true and faithful" marked a radical departure from previous paganism.

"Western civilization became prosperous, wealthy, advanced, and globally dominant with a worldview that allowed for the development of science and technology because of belief in an ordered cosmos of law-spheres, and similarly governed by deep moral conviction about objective standards of right and wrong," he remarked. "This led to learning, literacy, social stability, and civilization-building on a scale never seen before in the history of mankind."

However, the fruit of the West rejecting Christianity in favor of various ideologies – including secular humanism and Marxism – has been progressive cultural decay.

"When as a culture we no longer believe in creation and judgment in terms of the laws of God for His universe, we are steadily deconstructed downward into a void of meaninglessness," Boot added. "The Christian idea of a universe – unity in diversity – becomes a pagan pluralistic multiverse without ultimate order, structure, or design, and a growing nihilism is the result. In reaction, the modern state will try to invent pseudo-religious beliefs for the masses to keep people under control. Hence the new religion of climate, planetary salvation, and impending doom unless we are saved by the central planning and control of the new god of state."

God and Science

As secular governments struggle to remain coherent on the most basic tenets of human life – such as the definition of man and woman – the Frankfurt Declaration affirms that creation is ordered by objective truth, which mankind can learn through scientific observation.

We endorse science which seeks to discover, through the scientific method and debate, the truths that God has built into the natural world. We also affirm the limitations of science, including its inability to speak authoritatively on areas outside its purview and its propensity to err when data is lacking. Since man has fallen into sin, we further affirm that all his thoughts, deductions, and institutions contain degrees of corruption which tend to distort, manipulate, or suppress the truth.

The statement, however, rejects the weaponization of science for fearmongering or propaganda, notes that science is not sufficient to answer questions of ethics, and refutes the notion that man can be ideologically neutral.

Dr. James White – a pastor at Apologia Church in Mesa/Tempe, Arizona – told *The Daily Wire* that "the myth of neutrality" has hobbled Western evangelicalism and allowed for the cooperation of faith-based institutions with the lockdown regime.

"A consistent Christian understanding of the world begins with a recognition of God's creatorship and the fact that all of existence, universally, is defined by His purposes, His law, His final glory," White noted. "There is no neutral fact, for if it is a fact, God made it to be such."

White added that removing God from the picture leads to men filling the vacuum where only God should be.

"This likewise means that all of human inquiry, including scientific investigation, is an inquiry into the works of God, first and foremost, and hence cannot pretend neutrality," he continued. "If God has defined all things in creation, we will most certainly miss the true importance of creation if we pretend God can be made a side-issue rather than the central, defining reality."

Mankind As The Image Of God

The tradition of individual rights, equal justice under the law, and limited government in the Western world is rooted in the recognition of men as image-bearers of God. The Frankfurt Declaration affirms that such inalienable rights prevent the state from dehumanizing its people.

These rights and liberties include the right to corporate worship, personal and in-person relationships, vocational employments, and participation in the important events of human life such as the right to comfort the sick and the dying… to attend funerals, to witness the birth of one's child, to marry in a public gathering, to fellowship and eat together with others, and to engage in honorable work. We also affirm that governments should recognize that each individual is responsible for their own bodily well-being and should protect the right to personal medical self-determination.

The statement notes that lockdowns and mandates usurp the innate value of mankind by subjecting them to manipulation, enforced segregation, and other unjust deprivations of liberty.

Tobias Riemenschneider – the pastor of Evangelical Reformed Baptist Church in Frankfurt, Germany – told *The Daily Wire* that the modern Darwinian conception of mankind offers "no protection against the abuse of power by the stronger."

"We believe that we are now seeing the effects of the view of human beings that the states of the Western world have been promoting for many decades – namely, that human beings are nothing more than the product of an impersonal and ultimately purposeless evolutionary process without any transcendental meaning or value," Riemenschneider said. "According to the biblical worldview, on the other hand, God created man in His image and likeness, whereby all human beings have an inherent dignity and worth from which derive God-given, inalienable rights and liberties, that the state must respect and protect."

"When the state deprives a person of these rights and liberties or makes them contingent on the compliance with certain mandates, it dehumanizes them and makes them a mere object of state tyranny," he added. "For a lasting safeguard of our liberties, it is therefore necessary for the state to return to the Judeo-Christian view of God as the Creator of man, since only this provides the basis for the inalienable worth of each individual human being."

Limits of Authority

Legitimate earthly powers draw their authority – their right to be obeyed – from the God to whom all must give an account. Accordingly, the Frankfurt Declaration notes that the church and the state are granted limited authority only over their respective spheres.

God has delegated authority to civil governments for the purpose of rewarding good and punishing evil, and to protect the God-given rights and freedoms granted to all people. He has also delegated authority to the church in its various expressions, particularly to make disciples of all nations by preaching the Word of God, and to establish and administer redeemed communities of faith living under the authority of Christ.

The statement therefore rejects the tendency of governments to centralize beliefs or attempt to redefine good and evil – power grabs that disallow diversity of thought and conviction while conforming all citizens, particularly children, to approved state viewpoints.

Tim Stephens – the pastor of Fairview Baptist Church in Alberta, Canada – told *The Daily Wire* that secular governments view their decrees as "encompassing all of life."

"Worse than usurping their authority to carry out justice under the Lordship of Christ, they assume the place of God as Lawgiver, provider, and savior," he explained. "Trouble is, the government is a lousy savior with its interventions taking both responsibility and freedom from households and businesses to the detriment of all."

Stephens, who was jailed in a maximum-security facility last summer for resisting a lockdown order and opening his church, added that civil governments attract men who desire to use power for their own advantage.

"Without a knowledge of God, men seek to bring healing to the world apart from God's Savior, Jesus Christ. Today, men seek to control the climate, change human identity, and bring global peace through the power of human governments," Stephens observed. "However, these initiatives are leading to economic ruin, mutilated children, and increasing tyranny, along with conflict and division. The city of men failed at Babel, and it will fail again today."

CHRIST AS THE HEAD OF THE CHURCH

Christians recognize that Jesus Christ purchased His church and saved them from their sins through His substitutionary atonement on the cross. The Frankfurt Declaration therefore affirms that the church has the right – as defined by Jesus Himself – to worship in Spirit and Truth without unnecessary interference from the state.

We believe that Christ, who is Lord over all, calls all without distinction of any kind to freely and regularly gather together in His Name in local congregations to seek and serve Him in truth and love. We further affirm that the activities of the local church insofar as they are essential acts of worship are to be regulated by Christ alone.

The statement thus denies that secular governments are able to regulate the affairs of the church in matters of faith and practice.

Dr. John MacArthur – the senior pastor of Grace Community Church in Sun Valley, California – told *The Daily Wire* that earthly authorities have "always tended to view Christ as an adversary and an inconvenience."

"From Herod and Pontius Pilate until today, earthly governments have always sought to exert control over Christ and His kingdom," MacArthur explained. "Caesar is not content with the things that are Caesar's; he also wants control over the things that belong to God. So earthly rulers invariably try to seize as much dominance over the church as they can possibly appropriate."

MacArthur, whose church won a legal battle against California after officials attempted to mandate the cancellation of services, noted that unjust edicts – including those which support abortion, same-sex marriage, and the "barbaric, pagan mutilation of children" – represent a "formal, parliamentary declaration of war against God."

"The church's mission is not a partisan political one. There is no political solution to what ails our culture. The church's mission is to preach the gospel, recover souls from the domain of darkness, and train them to be Christ's disciples," MacArthur continued. "On the other hand, the more Caesar intrudes into matters that belong to Christ, the more the church must speak out on eternal and spiritual matters."

"We will continue to speak on such issues, and when government tries to silence the message or punish the messenger, we will not bow."

– PART 8 –

WHY I SIGNED THE FRANKFURT DECLARATION[1]

Dr. John MacArthur

CHRIST DECLARED, "My kingdom is not of this world... My kingdom is not of this realm." (John 18:36). Far from setting Himself up as a rival to Caesar, He was saying that the church belongs to a different, higher realm than any earthly government, and therefore she poses no threat to Caesar's *rightful* authority. The church's purpose is not to overthrow or usurp earthly governments. Jesus amplified that point when He said, "Render to Caesar the things that are Caesar's; and to God the things that are God's" (Matt. 22:21).

But for his part, Caesar has always tended to view Christ as an adversary and an inconvenience. From Herod and Pontius Pilate until today, earthly governments have always sought to exert control over Christ and His kingdom. Caesar is not content with the things that are Caesar's; he also wants control over the things that belong to God. So earthly rulers invariably try to seize as much dominance over the church as they can possibly appropriate.

Today's postmodern politicians are as determined as any government in history to intrude into matters that pertain to Christ. They impose moral standards that are hostile to biblical

---

1   The article was first published by Grace Church: https://www.grace-church.org/news/posts/3570.

principles. They use Caesar's bully pulpit to portray biblical values as a threat to the very existence of humanity. They champion and even subsidize those who want to indoctrinate children with overtly anti-Christian ideologies. They churn out executive orders, regulatory agencies, and arbitrary requirements that would hinder or halt the work of the church.

The Covid years simply made Caesar's strategy undeniably obvious. Government restrictions required churches to refrain from gathering while casinos and massage parlors were allowed to operate. Officials looked the other way when leftist protestors were given free rein to gather and even riot, but those same officials relentlessly worked to keep churches closed.

Obedience to such frivolous, heavy-handed government control would have required disobedience to Scripture. God clearly commands His people not to forsake their regular assembling for corporate worship (Heb. 10:25). And "we must obey God rather than men" (Acts 5:29). So we resumed our corporate worship, and that immediately unleashed the wrath of Caesar. Government agencies came after our church with every regulatory projectile they could hurl at us – legal demands, lawsuits, injunctions, and fines. They even threatened to expropriate our parking lot. Thankfully we prevailed in court – mainly, I believe, because the County of Los Angeles was not willing to let their health officials be deposed under oath.

Our triumph in that case came exactly a year before the Frankfurt Declaration was released. While the case was still in litigation, however, we released a statement of our own, titled, "Christ, not Caesar, Is Head of the church." What we stated then is in full agreement with the Frankfurt document.

The United States government (and others in the Western

world) have already established themselves as enemies of Christ by legalizing abortion; demanding that homosexuality be encouraged and celebrated; refusing to recognize God-given gender distinctions; sanctioning same-sex marriage; and promoting the barbaric, pagan mutilation of children. These overt government-sponsored attacks on long-established moral standards constitute a formal, parliamentary declaration of war against God, His created order, His moral law, and the authority of His Word. Our current government therefore now stands in opposition to God no less than the Baal-worshipers of the Old Testament did. Why would we not expect them to come after people who would put their lives on the line for the cause of God and His Word? There are many signs that sound churches and faithful believers are about to face a wave of harsh persecution.

The exposure of all this is a major problem for churches that have tried to compromise with the world. Some of them will simply deny the truth more openly. (Some are already doing that.) Those who will not compromise in order to mollify Caesar should sign the Frankfurt Declaration.

Christ and Caesar do operate in different realms. The church's mission is not a partisan political one. There is no political solution to what ails our culture. The church's mission is to preach the gospel, recover souls from the domain of darkness, and train them to be Christ's disciples. Christians must not be dissuaded from that task in order to achieve a mere temporal political objective. On the other hand, the more Caesar intrudes into matters that belong to Christ, the more the church must speak out on eternal and spiritual matters that the rest of the world wants to treat as merely "political." It is not the prerogative of Caesar to rewrite moral standards on matters like abortion, sexual perversion, gender roles, or other matters where Scripture has drawn clear lines. We will continue to speak on such issues, and when government tries to silence the message or punish the messenger, we will not bow.

"Whether it is right in the sight of God to give heed to you rather than to God, you be the judge; for we cannot stop speaking about what we have seen and heard" (Acts 4:19-20).

– Part 9 –

Why the Frankfurt Declaration Is Necessary
Tobias Riemenschneider

In the spring of 2021, pastors from different countries came together to draw up a joint declaration in response to the Covid measures enacted by many governments. The result is the Frankfurt Declaration of Christian and Civil Liberties, which was presented to the public on August 28, 2022, near Frankfurt, Germany. The document was initially signed by fifty pastors and theologians from America, the United Kingdom, Europe, Australia, and Africa, including men such as Grace Community Church pastor John MacArthur, African Christian University dean Voddie Baucham, and Apologia Church elder James White. In the meantime, more than 6,000 signatories from all over the world have joined the Frankfurt Declaration as of this writing.

Even though the concrete reason for drafting the Frankfurt Declaration was the totalitarian response to Covid, it is not primarily about these measures, but about the underlying spiritual reasons that led states to infringe so massively on the guaranteed rights of their citizens. The signatories of the Frankfurt Declaration see this unprecedented disregard for liberty as just one symptom of an emerging totalitarianism of the state over all spheres of society, including the church, that has developed for decades.

The Frankfurt Declaration seeks to address these threats with the timeless truths of God's Word through affirmations and denials derived from biblical principles.

Article 1: God the Creator as Sovereign Lawgiver and Judge

For centuries, the countries of the Western world have been moving further away from the biblical truth that God created the cosmos and everything in it, including man. Most people's thinking is now strongly influenced by a radical materialism assuming that all processes and phenomena in the world come from impersonal matter and motion rather than a personal and transcendent Creator.

But if there is no Creator God, then there is no divine lawgiver who has revealed His universal, immutable law to man, and there is no divine judge who at the end of time will judge all men according to this law. And if there is no heavenly lawgiver above the earthly state, then the state is the highest lawgiver, and its laws need not measure up to any higher standard. With no divine judge, human legislators need not consider answering to Him for their actions. The state and those who govern it thus assume for themselves the role of God, freely determining what is good and evil conduct without the bounds of a divine moral standard. The result is devastating: unconverted people, corrupt by nature, turn the commandments of God into their opposite, rebelliously calling good evil and evil good (Isa. 5:20).

Examples of this tendency during the Covid crisis abound. For example, the state decreed (even for healthy people) that visiting the elderly, the sick, and the dying was evil, although Christ says that such actions are signs by which one knows who is blessed of the Father and inherits the kingdom, and who is cursed and must depart from Christ into everlasting fire (Matt. 25:31-46). But the phenomenon of the state calling things good that have been considered sin for millennia is one we have been observing for years: the state enables divorce and sexual immorality, promotes homosexuality and transgenderism, and allows the killing of children in the womb.

The state both approves of such evils and demands that its citizens do likewise. Even kindergarteners are indoctrinated accordingly. Anyone who disagrees is considered backward, bigoted, hateful, and a threat to society.

The Frankfurt Declaration affirms that God, as supreme lawgiver and judge, is the ultimate source of ethics, and that He has revealed an unchanging morality which is rooted in His own character, and which determines for all people at all times what is good and evil conduct. It therefore denies that the state has the right to define morality and to demand unconditional obedience from its citizens when their beliefs contradict God's law, invoking the *clausula Petri*, that one ought to obey God rather than men (Acts 5:29).

Article 2: God as the Source of Truth and the Role of Science

With the turning away from the truth of the Creator God, other truths also increasingly falter. As Christians, we know that God has ordered creation by objective truths, which man can discover through scientific observation. This knowledge made scientific endeavors possible in the first place, since men once recognized that all scientific investigation is an inquiry into the works of God and hence cannot feign neutrality.

When science no longer serves to glorify God, then science itself becomes a god. Many today are convinced that science can provide answers to all questions and instructions for the right action in all situations. This scientism overlooks the fact that empirical inquiry may not only lead to erroneous results due to the lack of data and the human propensity for error, but that it can in no way provide answers to moral questions. Science can only say what is, but not what should be. Virology and epidemiology can say which measures might be promising to contain a virus, but they cannot answer whether a lockdown or other infringements on rights and liberties are ethically justified to achieve that goal.

However, this is exactly what happened during Covid: individual experts were considered to represent "science," and their predictions and recommendations guided the policies of entire governments. As C.S. Lewis once explained: "Let scientists tell us about sciences. But government involves questions about the good for man, and justice, and what things are worth having at what price; and on these a scientific training gives a man's opinion no added value."[1]

Since man has fallen into sin, all his thoughts, deductions and institutions contain degrees of corruption which tend to distort, manipulate, or suppress the truth. In the hands of ideologically driven people, truth becomes subject to change by reinterpretations, while science is quickly perverted into an instrument of in-

---

1   C.S. Lewis, "Willing Slaves of the Welfare State," first published in *The Observer*, July 20, 1958.

doctrination through fearmongering, propaganda, and the wielding of political power. Dissident voices are ignored, suppressed, or canceled. During Covid, dissenting doctors and scientists, some of whom had been considered luminaries in their field for decades, were silenced, discredited and sometimes dismissed from their jobs. But we see this trend in other areas as well. For example, the state and the "scientific consensus" have been propagating for decades that scientifically untenable theories, such as Darwinism, were settled truth. We are being told science has discovered that it is no longer possible to determine what a man or a woman is.

The Frankfurt Declaration endorses science which seeks to discover, through the scientific method and debate, the truths that God has built into the natural world, but it rejects scientism as the belief that science necessarily leads to truth and can provide answers to complex ethical questions. Furthermore, it denies that governments, scientific experts, or the media are morally and ideologically neutral and that their presentation of "the truth" should be trusted unconditionally.

Article 3: Mankind as the Image of God

If one no longer believes that there is a personal creator God, but that all processes are determined only by matter and motion, then man is nothing more than the product of an impersonal and ultimately purposeless evolutionary process without any transcendental purpose or value except to serve the "greater good" for society. The states of the Western world have promoted this view of man for decades, and we are now seeing its fruits: the Darwinian view of man offers no protection of the individual against the abuse of power by the stronger.

During the Covid crisis, states psychologically manipulated individuals by deliberately scaring them with predictions of horrific mortality rates and agonizing deaths by suffocation, as internal government papers show, and some governments have openly admitted.[2] Distrust of others was promoted by portraying them as potential threats to life and limb. Such propaganda enables many states to impose policies that infringed on people's rights and liberties in ways that previously seemed unthinkable in the "free" world. This happened even though such infringements are prohibited by the constitutions of most states.

To be clear: The issue is not whether or not certain measures make sense from a virological or epidemiological point of view, but whether or not the state has the right to forcefully impose such measures and thereby infringe on the liberties of its citizens.

According to the biblical worldview, on the other hand, God created man in His image and likeness, whereby all human beings have an inherent dignity and worth which serve as the grounds for God-given, inalienable rights, that the state must respect and protect (Rom. 13:3-4). These liberties include the right to in-person relationships, employment, medical self-determination, and participation in the important events of human life such as witnessing the birth of one's child, marrying in a public gathering, and fellowship with others. When the state deprives a person of these rights and liberties or makes them contingent on the compliance with certain mandates, citizens are dehumanized and

---

2   Florian Reiter, "'Wie bekommen wir Corona in den Griff?' Internes Papier aus Innenministerium empfahl, den Deutschen Corona-Angst zu machen," *Focus Online*, last modified April 11, 2020, https://www.focus.de/politik/deutschland/aus-dem-innenministerium-wie-sag-ichs-den-leuten-internes-papier-empfiehlt-den-deutschen-angst-zu-machen_id_11851227.html.

made a mere object of state tyranny. This is a direct attack on the image of God, which we have seen time and again, especially in anti-Christian systems like communism and socialism.

The Frankfurt Declaration therefore affirms the inalienable worth of every individual as made in the image of God and hence opposes the state's infringement on their God-given rights and liberties by lockdowns and mandates, which usurp the innate value of mankind by subjecting them to manipulation, enforced segregation, and other unjust deprivations of rights.

Article 4: God-Given Mandates and Limits of Authority

If one neither believes in a God who has supreme authority over all spheres of life, including the state, nor in human beings as created in the image of God, then the way is paved for the state to enact a totalitarian rule over all areas of life. In reaction to the growing nihilism that is the result of this turning away from the Christian faith, the modern state will try to invent pseudo-religious beliefs to keep people under control. Hence the new religion of multiculturalism, diversity, health, climate, planetary salvation, and impending doom unless we are saved by the central planning and control of the highest remaining power, the new god of state, which now assumes the role of ultimate lawgiver, provider, priest, and savior, thereby creating an authoritarian society in which the state is absolute.

In this system, dissidents cannot be tolerated because they threaten the narrative on which the legitimacy of this statism and totalitarianism is based. The state thus tries to centralize beliefs and conduct for its citizens. The state therefore has a special interest in gaining influence over children as early as possible in order to indoctrinate them according to the state ideology and turn them into "loyal" citizens, engendering an ideological intolerance which seeks to silence, cancel, re-educate, and punish those who disagree. We have seen this phenomenon not only with Covid, when the state elevated its narrative to absolute truth and deprived dissenters of the ability to even publicly express criticism through bans on demonstrations and unprecedented censorship in conventional and social media. Rather, we see a similar approach in a variety of other ideological narratives, such as feminism, sexual orientation and gender identity, or climate change.

However, it does not stop at the suppression of criticism; the state increasingly intervenes in all spheres of life to ensure behavior that conforms to the system. Thus, during Covid, the state intervened in the sphere of the family by prohibiting people from visiting and assisting family members or celebrating holidays, and it intervened in the sphere of the church by prohibiting believers from celebrating services, singing hymns, or administering the ordinances.

This totalitarian statism, however, is contrary to the divine order. All earthly powers draw their authority from God to whom all must give an account, and He has established different spheres of responsibility: the family, to whom the rod is given for training the children in the ways of the Lord; the church, to whom the Word is given for making disciples of all nations; and the state, to whom the sword is given for punishing evil and rewarding good. In doing so, God has at the same time set limits to the authority of these institutions.

The Frankfurt Declaration affirms that the family, the church, and the state are granted limited authority by God only over their respective spheres. It thus denies statism and totalitarian ideologies of governments which do not recognize the boundaries of their authority and usurp the mandates delegated by God to the church or the family.

Article 5: Christ as the Head of the Church

The fact that the state no longer recognizes the God-given limits of its authority and no longer has any fear of God is increasingly having an impact on the church. The state no longer recognizes the spiritual importance of the church but increasingly views and treats it like any other association or event, even as a danger to the states' own ideologies.

This mindset was clearly demonstrated during Covid. Whereas in the past churches were usually full during national emergencies because people understood that ultimately only God can save them (2 Chron. 7:13-14), this time worship services were banned for several weeks or months in large parts of the Western world. Once worship services were permitted again, they continued under severe restrictions, such as capacity limitations, distancing, mask or test requirements, or changes to the administration of the ordinances. The state even ordered the congregational singing of God's praises to be silenced throughout the country for several months. And sadly, most churches obeyed these mandates, many with full conviction, even defending the state's infringement on the church. We also saw pastors arrested or forced to answer in court for preaching the Word of God.

According to Scripture, however, the Lord Jesus Christ is the head of the church. He commands us not only to give to Caesar what belongs to Caesar, but also to give to God what belongs to God, thereby establishing the functional independence of the church from the state. The church must therefore refrain from submitting to an encroaching state when it orders that God be withheld His worship and praise, or that His blood-bought children be prevented from worshiping Him and receiving graces from the Word and ordinances free from state-imposed restrictions on access.

The Frankfurt Declaration affirms that the church belongs to the Lord Jesus Christ at the cost of His life and that it is accountable to Him alone in all matters of faith and practice. The activities of the local church, insofar as they are essential acts of worship, are therefore to be regulated by Christ alone. It denies that any other authority has jurisdiction over the church to criminalize, inhibit, or regulate any of its affairs in matters of faith and practice, or to relegate its activities to a non-essential status.

A Call for Respect, Repentance, and Resistance

The Frankfurt Declaration ends with an expression of gratitude to those civil authorities who respect these Christian beliefs and the rights and liberties of each individual, and with a call to repentance to those civil authorities who have disregarded these freedoms, lest in the abuse of their God-given authority they become liable to God's wrath. It also encourages Christians to steadfastly and faithfully obey the Lord rather than men and stand by one another while praying that God would give us the grace to remain faithful and persevere to the end.

The Frankfurt Declaration is not a politicization of the gospel, quite the contrary, nor is it a call for strife and division in the church or unlawful rebellion against the state. It is meant to provide light and strength for Christians for a faithful witness to Jesus Christ in our time. May God graciously use it in this way for His glory.

– PART 10 –

(How to) Love Your Neighbor – The BioLogos Statement vs. The Frankfurt Declaration: Two Opposite Evangelical Responses to the State's Power[1]

Jacob Reaume

THE STATES' RESPONSES TO COVID-19 intersected with church practices in varying degrees, and pastors had to respond to individual state mandates without forewarning and often under intense pressure. With the COVID-19 measures now phased out, we can soberly reflect on the responses in order to gain wisdom for the future. Two polarizing responses emerged among Evangelicals, and they are worth comparing.

One group equated the civil governments' agenda with Christ's agenda, as represented in BioLogos' "Love Your Neighbor, Get the Shot: A Christian Statement on Science for Pandemic Times."[2] Another group differentiated between Christ's agenda and the states' agenda, as represented in "The Frankfurt Decla-

---

1 The article was published by *Christ Over All*: https://christoverall.com/article/concise/the-biologos-statement-vs-the-frankfurt-declaration-two-opposite-evangelical-responses-to-the-states-power/.

2 "Love Your Neighbor, Get the Shot: A Christian Statement on Science for Pandemic Times," *BioLogos*, https://statement.biologos.org.

ration of Christian and Civil Liberties." In what follows, I will compare the two statements in order to show that the BioLogos Statement is an attempt to synthesize Christianity with the course of this world during the COVID-19 era, whereas the Frankfurt Declaration places Christianity in antithesis to the spirit of the age during the COVID-19 era. By contrasting these two statements, my hope is that Christians will grow wise to recognize and resist a syncretistic form of "Christianity" that loses its biblical potency.

1. Who Has Ultimate Authority?

The two statements fundamentally differ in where each locates its ultimate authority. The BioLogos statement gives credence to "the authority of God's Word," but in the same sentence, immediately after this, it affirms "science as a tool to understand God's world." So where does the authority ultimately rest?

The thrust of the document is found in the next sentence: "We call on all Christians to follow the advice of public health experts and support scientists doing crucial biomedical research on COVID-19." The authority of God's Word has little bearing on the mandates other than to convince Christians to follow them, even insisting that Dr. Fauci "should be listened to."

In contrast, the Frankfurt Declaration's preamble confesses the "timeless truths of God's Word," but it does not mention science until Article 2, in which it defines science as a tool to discover truths in "the natural world." Unlike the BioLogos Statement, however, the Frankfurt Declaration creates two crucial categories: science as a tool, and "scientism" as an ideology that "ignores or suppresses the concerns of dissident voices" while attempting to control "complex social realities." In other words, science is the discovery of truth, and scientism is a political agenda under the pretense of science. The bulk of the Frankfurt Declaration demonstrates that Scripture and scientism are antithetical sources of authority, whereas the BioLogos Statement, conflating science with scientism, presents Scripture as demanding compliance with scientism.

2. Humanity's Capacity for Sin

Underneath so many wrong beliefs is an insufficient understanding of the nature of humanity, and, in this case, an understanding of mankind's capacity for sin. The BioLogos Statement acknowledges that state abuses of science and medicine have occurred in the past, but undergirding the BioLogos Statement is the profound presupposition that similar misdeeds could not happen in the response to COVID-19. Synthesizing Scripture with scientism, the BioLogos Statement dismisses notions that COVID-19 responses could be in serious error or stem from nefarious intent. It accuses detractors of vilifying scientists while ignoring their findings, and generalizes them as believing in "conspiracy theories that go viral." It grants that "thoughtful Christians may disagree on public policy," framing disagreements as trivial matters of opinion, while emphasizing that "none of us should ignore clear scientific evidence." With COVID-19, "Christians should listen to scientists and doctors…especially when millions of lives are at stake."

The Frankfurt Declaration recognizes humanity's continuing capacity for sin, contrasting Scripture with the claims that Christians should trust policymakers: "Since man has fallen into sin, we further affirm that all his thoughts, deductions, and institutions contain degrees of corruption which tend to distort, manipulate, or suppress the truth," and, "We therefore deny that human governments are morally and ideologically neutral…and that their narrative should be unconditionally trusted." The Frankfurt Declaration assumes the fallen nature of men who direct policy and oversee science, whereas the BioLogos Statement assumes that they should be trusted, especially in civil governments' response to COVID-19.

3. On Church Gatherings

The difference is explicit in how the two statements interact with policies that bear on gathered Christian worship. The BioLogos Statement notes, "Even closer to our hearts is the impact of quarantine on church fellowship." Compare that to the Frankfurt Declaration: "We believe that Christ, who is Lord over all, calls all without distinction of any kind to freely and regularly gather together in His Name in local congregations to seek and serve Him in truth and love." The former subjectivizes worship as something close to our hearts, whereas the latter presents worship objectively as a gathering mandated by Christ.

The BioLogos Statement then calls Christians to negotiate worship with public health policies, policies that, without qualification, it equates with protecting the vulnerable: "Christians need to balance God's call to meet together with God's call to protect the vulnerable among us." It tenders the limitations or cessation of gathered worship as a "call to sacrifice ourselves for others and accept temporary limitations on our freedom." Just the reverse, the Frankfurt Declaration presents gathered worship as exclusively designed by God for God: "We further affirm that the activities of the local church insofar as they are essential acts of worship are to be regulated by Christ alone," and, "We thus repudiate all actions of the State that ... regulate any of its activities which are undertaken as acts of service toward its Lord."

The BioLogos Statement locates the impetus for worship in the hearts of believers, calls for a compromise between God's call to worship and the state mandates, and presents alterations to worship as personal sacrifice. Quite the opposite, the Frankfurt Declaration locates the impetus for worship in the demands of Christ, calls for exclusive obedience to Him amidst pressure to compromise, and declares that worship is nonnegotiable because it belongs to Christ. The BioLogos Statement synthesizes Christian worship with the COVID-19 response, and the Frankfurt Declaration places worship as its antithesis.

4. Definitions of Faith and Fear

The gulf between these statements widens further when definitions of faith amidst fear are postulated. To the BioLogos Statement, faith finds its expression in resolutions to "wear masks in indoor public places and follow other physical distancing rules given by public health officials," "get vaccinated," "correct misinformation and conspiracy theories" – in context, that means correcting dissident views – and "work for justice for communities who suffered the most deaths from COVID-19," which includes "the elderly in nursing homes, the Navajo nation...and people of color." Each resolution is an expression of the spirit of the age, not one is grounded in explicit scriptural commands, and some of them (masks, social distancing, vaccinations) are inconclusive on whether they actually stop the spread of Covid. The call to work for justice might have the air of being scriptural, but, in this case, it is an unscriptural collectivist view of justice, emphasizing the perceived rights of groups instead of the God-given rights of individuals.

Like the BioLogos Statement, the Frankfurt Declaration concludes with a call to courage amidst fear, but unlike the BioLogos Statement it is a call to obey God when the world demands otherwise. Referencing the Hebrews' refusal to obey the order to worship Nebuchadnezzar's golden statue in Dan. 3:16, the Frankfurt Declaration reads, "To those who desire to compel us to obey the secular State rather than God, we respectfully but firmly say… 'We have no need to answer you in this matter.'" The Frankfurt Declaration calls on states that violate Scripture "to repent and to become again the protectors of liberty and of the rights that God has given to all men, lest in the abuse of your God-given authority, you become liable to God's wrath."

In sum, the BioLogos Statement calls for Christians to obey the state, but the Frankfurt Declaration calls for states and individuals to obey Christ above all. Each presents itself as a call to courage, but the actions required are poles apart.

5. Summary and Takeaway

In the end, each statement embodies conflicting responses that emerged among Evangelicals during the COVID-19 crisis – responses that stem from a larger understanding of ultimate authority, humanity, biblical commands, and even faith and fear itself. The BioLogos Statement attempted to synthesize Christianity with the government's response to COVID-19, putting obedience to Christ in lockstep with obedience to the state. The Frankfurt Declaration declared that Christ is over the state, the church, and individuals, with the result that Christians in certain cases disobey the government's response to COVID-19.

With the pressures of the crisis beyond us, we can soberly evaluate how churches responded to the COVID-19 mandates and lockdowns. Our society and civil governments, increasingly influenced by godless ideologies, are often incapable of discerning good from evil, and they regularly confuse the two, even in times of relatively low pressure. In times of high pressure, as in a perceived public health emergency, we should anticipate the compounding of their confusion. Turning to them for direction seems like a good decision, but ultimately Christians must heed the voice of God in Scripture, believing that He is our supreme standard in all things. A failure to heed Scripture, no matter how sincere, is still a failure. The failure is compounded when Evangelicals compromise away gathered worship and the right of King Jesus to rule His church – all in the name of allegiance to Christ, love of neighbor, and the public good. Such refusal to heed Scripture is not merely failure or even compounded failures, but it is in fact sin.

– Part 11 –

Address at the "Church at War" Conference in Waterloo, ON, Canada

Tobias Riemenschneider

I AM VERY GRATEFUL to be here, among my Canadian brothers and sisters in Christ. It is a great privilege and honor for me to be able to speak to you. When I contacted Pastor Jacob Reaume two weeks ago and asked him if it was still possible to attend the conference, he told me that it was completely sold out but that he would build a balcony for me if necessary and his church would pay the conference fee and hotel for me. I am overwhelmed by the love and generosity of my dear brother Jacob and his church, and I praise God for that.

I want to use the short time I have to encourage you by telling you what effect your faithfulness has had on me personally and the church in Germany. The situation in Germany was pretty much the same as in Canada. We had lockdowns, social distancing, mask mandates, and so on. Even singing praises to the Lord was forbidden for several months. And our rulers and media openly expressed their hatred for the unvaccinated. They even planned to introduce vaccine mandates for the entire population. It was a time of distress and fear like I had never experienced before. And most churches just went along with everything and believed everything. They even turned on their own sheep when they did not want to comply with everything. The Protestant State Church even started a campaign, "Vaccinate your neighbor as yourself." Our church did not comply. We did not surrender to Caesar what belonged to God. But we tried to do everything secretly and hoped that no one would find out about us.

But then I heard that Pastor James Coates had been arrested for having church. And something changed in my heart. I was overwhelmed with love for my brother, whom I had never heard of, and I wept and prayed for him and his family – and I was angry at the sheer injustice. Actually, you can see how I felt. There is video on the Internet showing Pastor Jacob Reaume preaching to his flock, crying and shouting with tears that Pastor James has been jailed. There you can see exactly how I felt too.

And then Pastor Tim Stephens was arrested. I could barely watch the video of him being ripped from the arms of his crying children. It broke my heart. Then Pastor Steve Richardson lost his job because he stood up for the truth, for his flock, and for his Lord.

But all this did not make me more fearful, but – on the contrary – made me courageous. I thought, "If my brothers in Canada go to jail and are fined and lose their jobs, I can at least take a public stand." So, I wrote a statement on how the church should respond biblically to the restrictions. And this statement was shared throughout Germany and even translated into other languages, including English. This was followed by another statement and a sermon on Romans 13. We then formed a group of pastors to join forces. We organized prayer days to pray for an end to this tyranny. In August, we had a conference where we looked back at two and a half years of Covid. I also co-authored the Frankfurt Declaration, which was signed by these pastors here and which you can also read and sign at frankfurtdeclaration.com.

I am not telling you this to boast with what I did during Covid. I was a scared little worm. But by the grace of God, I became courageous. And God used these pastors here to make me courageous and be a comfort for many Christians in Germany. God used your suffering, the suffering of these pastors, to bless and encourage his people on the other side of the world.

I have a request for all of you: honor these men. Pray for them. Support them, even financially. Stand up for them. Fight for them. As they have done for you. And I know this may sound harsh, but if you are in a church with a pastor who was a coward during Covid, who was not manly and strong and courageous, and who has not repented, please consider becoming part of the flock of one of these pastors here. They have proven their faithfulness. And that is what you will need in the days ahead: a faithful pastor who is willing to pay fines, lose his job, and go to jail for you. Thank you. Amen.

Ingram Content Group UK Ltd.
Milton Keynes UK
UKHW020726300523
422560UK00013B/284